# Edible
# Container
# Gardening
*for*
# Canada

D0323984

*Rob Sproule*

Lone Pine Publishing

**Lone Pine Publishing**
2311 – 96 Street
Edmonton, AB T6N 1G3
Canada
Website: www.lonepinepublishing.com


**Library and Archives Canada Cataloguing in Publication**

Sproule, Rob, 1978-
   Edible container gardening for Canada / Rob Sproule.

Includes index.
ISBN 978-1-55105-890-0

   1. Container gardening--Canada.  I. Title.

SB418.S665 2013        635.9'860971        C2012-907638-4

*Editorial Director:* Nancy Foulds
*Project Editor:* Sheila Quinlan
*Production Manager:* Gene Longson
*Layout and Design:* Janina Kuerschner
*Production Support:* Greg Brown
*Cover Design:* Gerry Dotto

*Photo Credits:* All photos are by Rob Sproule except: Dora Berry 9, 10, 19, 108b; Tamara Eder 121; Chad Kile 249a&b; Megan Mundell-Hahn 6, 7, 11, 12, 14, 17, 18, 23, 29, 30, 32, 40, 41, 47g, 48, 49, 51b, 54a, 55c, 56, 57, 61a, 62c, 64, 65, 71a,c&d, 72, 76b, 80, 88, 89, 94a, 95g, 96, 97, 103d&f, 105, 111b, 112, 114a, 116, 117, 118b, 122a, 123b, 124, 127b&c, 128, 129, 133a,e&f, 134, 137a&f, 138, 139, 140, 141, 142, 143(all), 144, 145, 146, 147a, 148, 151a&c, 152, 153, 155a&d, 156, 158a, 159a, 163a&f, 167c, 169, 171a&d, 172, 173, 174, 175b, 176, 178b, 179a, 184, 185, 186a, 187e, 189, 190, 192, 193, 195a&b, 197b&d, 198, 200a&b, 201h, 208e, 210, 211, 212b, 213d, 215, 217a&c, 219, 221b, 222, 225f, 226, 228a, 229b,d&e, 250, 251a&b, 252, 258, 259b, 260, 262a&b, 263a&b, 264, 265a&b, 272; Angela Neuman 69a; Anna Pandos 28, 149; Pickering Nurseries 87a; Plant World 59a, 74, 91, 99a; Proven Winners 61b; Renee's Garden 15, 24, 37, 43b, 44, 52, 60a&b, 68, 69b, 76a, 77, 79c&d, 92, 99b, 100, 102c, 107, 108a, 111d, 115f, 118a, 122b, 125, 132a, 136a&b, 147b, 154, 159c, 166, 170, 171c, 191a&e, 206b, 207a, 208a, 212a, 216, 220, 223, 224; Nanette Samol 55a, 150, 159g; Paul Swanson 155b; Sandy Weatherall 137g; Wikimedia Commons 115e (Averette@en.wikipedia), 183e (E.nielsen), 196a (Tom Maack), 196b (Harry Peterson-Nedry), 197c (Elena Chochkova).

We acknowledge the financial support of the Government of Canada through the Canada Book Fund (CBF) for our publishing activities.

*PC:* 16

# CONTENTS

# DEDICATION

To new generations of gardeners.

# ACKNOWLEDGEMENTS

First and foremost, thanks to my beloved wife Megan Mundell-Hahn, my mentor, inspiration and amazing photographer. You're the reason everything is possible.

Thanks to my business partners and family, namely Bob, Dave and Adam Sproule, for giving me the time I needed to write this.

This book took a village. Most of the mixed containers I featured had to be grown from scratch, so I converted part of the Salisbury Greenhouse into a "workshop" where I spent many happy hours experimenting and discovering. Throughout six months of planning and maintaining, my fellow Salisbury-ites lent many hands through advice, planting, moving, weeding and more. A special thanks to Mario Salazar, Yong Hoon Cho, Brett Kerley, Tony Lucardie, Angela Neuman, Alison Beck, Dylan Chase, Matt Petram and Doug Johnson.

In order to show readers what they could do with these plants in the kitchen, as well as the garden, I put out a request for people to send pictures of how they used their garden-grown edibles. Thanks to Renee Shepherd of Renee's Garden seed company, Dora Berry, Alison Beck, Mario Salazar and Michelle Dixon for answering the call. Thanks also to Justine Baamann and family for your time and dedication.

Finally, thanks to the people who opened their yards so that Meg could take her wonderful pictures: Val MacMillan, Cindy Mundell, Lynn Parker, Luella Chmelyk and Megan Bertagnolli. Thanks also to Fern and the gang at Toronto Balconies in Bloom for their great project.

It's exhilarating to work on the exploding trend that is edible container gardening. I travelled across Canada this summer and met some amazing people who are spearheading edible gardening projects across Canada, including the following, from west to east:

**Renee's Garden**
www.reneesgarden.com
*Special thanks to Renee Shepherd.*

**The Teahouse**
Ferguson Point, Stanley Park
Vancouver, BC
www.vancouverdine.com/teahouse
*Special thanks to Annubelle Leslie.*

**Fairmont Waterfront**
900 Canada Place Way
Vancouver, BC
www.fairmont.com/
waterfront-vancouver
*Special thanks to Michael King.*

**Minter Gardens**
52892 Bunker Road
Chilliwack, BC
www.mintergardens.com
*Special thanks to Brian Minter.*

**Leaf & Lyre Urban Farms**
1418-7 Avenue NW
Calgary, AB
www.leafandlyre.com
*Special thanks to Chad Kile
and Rod Olson.*

**Salisbury Greenhouse**
& Landscaping
52337 Range Road 232
Sherwood Park, Alberta
www.salisburygreenhouse.com
*Special thanks to the entire staff.
I'm privileged to be able to work
alongside you.*

**Edmonton Valley Zoo**
13315 Buena Vista Road
Edmonton, AB
www.edmonton.ca/valleyzoo
www.buildingourzoo.com
*Special thanks to Barbara Chapman and
the Valley Zoo Development Society,
Denise Prefontaine, Dean Treichel, Robyn
Kunimoto, Wade Krasnow, Greg Lalonde
and Laura Gausman.*

**Muttart Conservatory**
9626-96A Street
Edmonton, AB
www.edmonton.ca/muttart

**Wellington Garden Centre**
13648-142 Street
Edmonton, AB
www.wellingtongardencentre.com

**FoodShare Toronto**
90 Croatia Street
Toronto, ON
www.foodshare.net
*Special thanks to Mary Roufail, Jeanny
Gonzalez, Cheryl Douglass, Sophia
Ilyniak and Justin Nadeau.*

**Fairmont Royal York**
100 Front Street W
Toronto, ON
www.fairmont.com/royal-york-toronto
*Special thanks to Catherine Tschannen
and Andrew Court.*

**Toronto Botanical Garden**
777 Lawrence Avenue E
Toronto, ON
www.torontobotanicalgarden.ca

**Plant World Garden Centre**
4000 Eglinton Avenue W
Etobicoke, ON
www.plantworld.net

**Rooftop Gardens Project**
Alternatives.ca
3720 avenue du Parc
Montreal, QC
www.alternatives.ca
*Special thanks to Gaëlle Janvier.*

**Montreal Botanical Garden**
4101 rue Sherbrooke Est
Montreal, QCwww.ville.montreal.qc.ca/
jardin/en/menu

# INTRODUCTION

**IT'S EXCITING TO WRITE** a book that is the first of its kind. With the explosion of interest in home-grown food, there is a multitude of new books on how to do it, with a few of them even focusing on container gardening. This is the first book (that I know of) dedicated to designing mixed containers using only edible herbs, vegetables, fruits and flowers.

It's a nasty myth that you can't be just as creative and artistic with containers full of mixed edibles as you can be with mixed annuals.

As with anything original, this book took a long time to put together. I knew that before I could write about designing containers with mixed edibles, I had to grow each one as a trial. By the time pen went to paper (or rather, first key stroke was entered into word processor), hundreds of hours had already gone into conceiving, planning, researching, ordering, designing and planting over 100 mixed containers using hundreds of different ingredients. Those that didn't thrive became grazing fodder while the best of them are represented here. I couldn't have done it alone, as the long thank-you list on the previous pages illustrates.

I'm very excited to be sharing the results of my labour with you. To me, these recipes are a tantalizing glimpse of what I believe edible gardening to be evolving into. My goal for this project is to both educate and inspire: too much education and you have a textbook; too much inspiration and you have pretty pictures that no one will think they can replicate. I hope that this book shows you what is possible, educates you on how to do it and inspires you to get your hands dirty and take control of your own food supply. Food, after all, is what this is all about. If reading this book makes you plant a container or two of veggies on the front patio this season, I've done my job.

## The Changing Face of Gardening

Many scholars argue that the beginning of human civilization as we know it didn't happen with fire, the wheel or cities, but with the planting of seeds. The ancient empires of Mesopotamia, Egypt and the Aztecs began when people stayed in one place long enough to put seeds in the ground and wait until they matured into life-sustaining crops. Our civilization began with gardening, and today the desire to grow plants remains one of the most elemental drives we have.

What makes gardening most fascinating is that it is as contemporary as it is ancient. While the timeless desire to grow remains constant, the ways in which we express that desire vary according to the traditions we've learned and the trends that catch our interest.

The contemporary face of gardening is a lot like fashion: it's all about colour, and the styles change every season. Staged container gardens splash across glossy magazines, and spring television commercials proclaim the revolutionary magnificence of this or that new product. As a garden centre owner, I spend a lot of my time looking into a proverbial crystal ball and trying to predict the next big thing. One year it's the colour purple and the next it might be white.

The author in his "workshop" at Salisbury Greenhouse, where most of the planters in this book were conceived and nurtured.

A lot of people have asked me if the explosion in popularity of growing food is just a trend that will dissipate in the coming years. I tell them, definitively, no. The desire to grow food is much more fundamental than trends ever are. It's a deeply seated shift in perspective in what people want from their gardens and how they define gardening itself. A new generation of gardeners who want their children to grow up knowing where their food comes from is at the spearhead of the change.

## What I've Included and Not Included

Writing about plants is a humbling experience. Many of the species I encounter, especially edibles, have histories that are as expansive and complex as those of many nations. It's always a challenge not sounding like a history professor with patches on my elbows.

Throughout this book I've tried to include historically significant edibles wherever I could. The plants we've eaten throughout the millennia have helped shape our cultural and national identities in powerful ways. As new generations of Canadians drive the evolution of edible gardening forward, I think it's important to remember that plants such as olives and corn were the vehicles that helped pushed our civilization forward.

I mustered together hundreds of varieties of edibles, and while I experimented with combining all of them, only the best mixes made it into print.

## The Benefits of Growing Your Own Food

The fascinating thing about the explosion of interest in home-grown food, and what defines it as more fundamental than other trends, is that different groups of people have different motivations for doing it. Here are just a few that I've come across while talking to people about it.

### For Your Health

For how enjoyable gardening is, many people are surprised to find out how healthy it is. Numerous studies have linked it to lower risk of diabetes, heart disease and stroke. A study by the University of Arkansas even found that gardeners had lower rates of osteoporosis than people who did other kinds of exercise, like jogging or aerobics.

Gardening ranges from low intensity (light planting or weeding) to high intensity (heavy lifting and pulling) exercise. Unlike exercises such as jogging or weight-training, which tend to focus on specific muscle groups, gardening includes so many types of activity that it usually provides a well-balanced workout. A study by the University of Iowa found that moderate intensity activities, such as planting, pruning or weeding, burn about 200 calories for men and about 150 for women in 30 minutes of gardening. Another advantage gardening has over many other exercises is that you don't need to leave your yard to do it. There are no membership fees or rows of treadmills.

The amount of calories we burn may be the most quantifiable health benefit of gardening, but it's certainly not the only one. The pride we feel after an hour of good gardening ripples through our lives and improves our mental health in countless ways. Gardeners tend to sleep better after having spent their evenings in the fresh air of their garden instead of on the couch in front of a TV screen. They also tend to approach their daily challenges with a more positive, constructive and confident outlook.

You don't need to dedicate copious space to grow edibles; a corner of the deck will yield a surprising harvest.

When I think of the magic of gardening, I often think of Joan Baker, a beloved family friend who lives in Cardiff, Wales. Joan is 89 years old. She lives alone and keeps a stunning garden that is a privilege to walk through. She's an internationally acclaimed artist and swears that her garden is the secret to her energy.

Gardening connects us to the earth. Feeling moist soil between our fingers nourishes us in ways impossible to measure. It yields rewards far above eating fresh tomatoes or burning calories. It reaffirms our connection with nature and, in doing so, our place within it.

Growing food is magical to kids. Here, Sofia Berry shows off her crabapple harvest.

Canadians spend about four hours a day watching television. If we took a half-hour out of each of those four-hour chunks and spent it in the garden, we'd be rewarded with a healthier lifestyle and a more positive state of mind.

### For the Kids

It's no surprise to anyone that we're in the midst of an epidemic of childhood obesity and diabetes, conditions that stem largely from a lack of exercise and poor eating habits. But there is a bright side. At the greenhouse I meet young families who are dedicated to raising their children with an appreciation for growing plants, eating fresh vegetables and the magic of nature overall. Teaching your children how to grow peas and tomatoes doesn't cost anything, and the rewards will echo throughout their lives.

Dora and Patrick Berry live on a mature street just outside of Edmonton. They are a young family with two beautiful daughters. Dora is a full-time mom who spends as much time in the garden with Sofia and Vienna as possible. She told me that she wants them to have "an appreciation for gardening, for growing their own fruits and vegetables, and to learn how plants grow."

My generation (I was born in 1978) grew up during a period of massive technological change. We understand that while things like the internet have many benefits, they can also isolate us from the wonders of the natural world. As we have our own families, many young parents are turning off the flashing screens and taking the kids outside.

Young parents are notoriously busy as they balance the expectations of careers with the needs of their children. Dora insists that gardening with your kids doesn't have to take a lot of time, saying that although turning off the TV and getting into the garden sounds intimidating, "all you need is soil, a pot and some seeds and you'll have so much fun."

Dora wants her daughters to grow up feeling connected to the earth. She says it's about "education and knowledge, but it's also for the health benefits of getting outside, breathing fresh air and being surrounded by plants. Sofia loves mixing soil and watching the leaves, flowers and fruit develop on the plants."

The Baamanns, who hang their hat in Thunder Bay, are another inspiring young family. Justine and Iwan are raising their two girls, Ruthie and Asher, to appreciate the value of growing their own food. Justine tells me that it's important for them to see the source of their food. "There's nothing like seeing your hard work pay off and showing them the carrots that they planted as tiny seeds," she says.

Justine is battling the stereotype that an edible garden needs to be "a gigantic garden like your Grandma had." She grows a variety of unusual edibles, including purple carrots, yellow raspberries and unique tomatoes, and tells me that the best part of it all is "watching your kids' delight in pulling up their very own carrots, picking their own berries or munching on some fresh tomatoes."

Justine and her daughter Ruthie admire some pansies. Justine wants Ruthie to grow up knowing the value of growing food.

## For the Wallet

Even with all the health benefits of growing food, one of the largest factors in its explosion in popularity is undoubtedly economic. In 2008, the U.S. and Canada were hit by a recession that devastated families and made us all ask ourselves whether or not, if we lost our jobs, we had the skills we needed to support ourselves and our families on very little income. Knowing how to grow a vegetable garden is a big part of financial self-sufficiency, and since the recession a lot of people have taken it upon themselves, either from necessity or to be prepared, to learn.

Growing food really is like growing money. By planting some seeds and investing a little bit of time and effort, a family can save hundreds of dollars on the grocery bill. The varieties you grow have a lot to do with how much money you save. You're not going to harvest enough olives off an olive tree to break even, but vegetables such as beans, tomatoes, potatoes and carrots are like high-interest investments. If you're budget minded, look for varieties in this book that have a "feet" icon beside them. This means both that they are easy to find and that they tend to be on the lower end of the money scale.

Growing your own food will save money on the grocery bill.

## Most Commonly Asked Questions

Garden centres are the front lines of the rapidly changing world of gardening, where beginners and experts alike come to browse, mingle and chat about their ideas and inspirations. It's through my daily conversations with gardeners that I learn which plants are popular, what the trends actually are (don't always believe the gardening magazines) and get a feel of the general gardening zeitgeist.

Lately the questions have taken a distinct turn toward edibles. While "what goes with purple?" will always be asked, "what kinds of beans need a trellis?" and "how much sun does spinach need?" have become staples as well. The people asking them are usually younger and, more often than not, both excited and nervous about the new experiment they are about to try. I'm always happy to reassure them that it's not as hard as they think.

For each of the hundreds of the herb, vegetable, fruit and edible flower varieties I discuss in this book, I've provided four icons that address the questions most commonly asked about them. These are meant not only

My workshop in spring, full of tomatoes and planting experiments among the pots of annuals.

to provide a quick reference for you, but also to allow me, in the limited space I have, to get on to the juicy stuff about how to use the plant. The icons will give you answers to these four questions: how much sun does it need?; how much water does it need?; how easy is it to find?; and how hard is it to take care of?

## Question #1: Exposure

The magic of plants is in their ability to transform from a seed, to a plant, to producing buckets of apples, strawberries or beans using only nutrients from the soil below and energy from the sun above. The fact that edible plants are able to perform such alchemy, often in one growing season, means that, as a rule of thumb, they need a lot of sun. No edible plant can do its job in the shade; it would be like asking a marathon runner to run without protein. That being said, there is still a wide variation in the conditions in which plants thrive.

You'll find that the containers in this book constitute a United Nations of edible plants. We live in a time wherein herbs, veggies and fruits from around the world are available to us with a drive down the street or a click of the mouse. The variety of climatic regions our edibles come from makes it important to recognize and accommodate their heat and sun tolerances.

A plant will be more likely to thrive if it's planted in a spot that mimics the conditions where it has evolved

Not all herbs like it hot and dry. Vietnamese fish mint is native to swamps, so it prefers partial sun and lots of water.

Peas are a cool-weather crop and don't like midsummer heat.

and grown for thousands of years; that's why I endeavour to tell you where the plant is from. If you have a fiery south exposure then you might choose a plant from the open Australian scrub-land, or if your yard is sunny but the light is dappled under trees, you might want to choose European woodland plants.

Edible plants react to air temperature just as much as sunlight. Cool-weather plants, like Chinese greens, spinach and carrots, tend to get bitter or go straight to flower if exposed to the scorching July temperatures that tomatoes and corn thrive on. I'll never give cool-loving veggies a "sun with no cloud" rating, and I will indicate where it's best to grow a certain crop in early spring and a different, heat-loving crop in summer.

I will often make caveats for different exposure levels in different parts of the country. Canada is a massive country with hundreds of climatic regions within it. The most important factor for our purposes is the intensity of the sunlight. Although more humid areas of the country, namely those near the coast and as far inland as southern Ontario and central BC, can get very hot, the high humidity tempers the sun's intensity so that more plants can handle more exposure. The geographic centre of Canada, namely the Prairies and NWT, are cooler but drier, so the sun is very intense. Some plants that thrive in the full sun of humid regions will potentially wilt or burn on the Prairies. I will warn you if full exposure plants are not suitable for dry heat.

The more heat and sunlight you give tomatoes, the more they will reward you. Just keep the hose handy; they need a lot of moisture to make juicy tomatoes.

Each plant will get one of three symbols.

This means that the plant needs at least six hours of good sunlight to perform at its best. Less sunlight will probably cause its original compact, pleasing habit to get leggy and its foliage to turn a paler shade of green. This category includes many popular edibles such as tomatoes, corn and zucchini. Without significant sun you may see lower yields and under-sized fruit. Full-sun plants are ideal for your south-facing deck or patio, under the white siding that reflects the sun.

 A sun with partial cloud cover indicates a plant that needs a good amount of sun but will have to be protected from the afternoon sun. Exposure to morning sun is perfect for these plants, but they will typically also be good in dappled afternoon sun (e.g., south exposure but sheltered by large trees) or evening sun. Many cool-weather plants, such as carrots and lettuce, fall into this category.

Clouds indicate edibles that need to be sheltered. These plants are typically good for areas that receive partial sun, but they can tolerate less. There aren't very many edibles in this category because sunlight is such an important part of food production.

### Question #2: Moisture

The amount of water a plant gets is arguably the most determining factor in its development. As with sunlight, the amount of water a plant needs is largely a product of its native land. Root systems evolve in response to the amount of water that is available, and if a plant gets a dramatically different amount of water than what it needs or is accustomed to over a sustained period, the roots won't be able to properly deal with it and the plant will suffer. The droplet symbol is designed to tell you how much water your plant needs to perform at its best.

Edible plants typically need a consistent supply of moisture to perform at their best. This can be a challenge in the cramped, hot quarters of container gardens. Many of the varieties that demand consistent moisture, such as tomatoes and cucumbers, come from the tropics, where their roots have evolved to grow near the soil surface. In Canada, and especially in dry air regions like the Prairies, you may need to water every day—sometimes even twice a day—to keep your plants happy.

One droplet means that the plant is drought tolerant and is more likely to appreciate sandy, very well-draining soils. Drought tolerant plants don't like to be plunked into large containers; often the pot in which you buy it will suffice for the season. If you transplant it into a large container, make sure the medium drains freely.

Many herbs are drought tolerant.

Allow the surface of the soil to dry visibly between waterings, but remember that it's not healthy for any plant to wilt. If you plant in a peat moss–based mix, water it when the medium pulls slightly away from the sides of the container, indicating that the spongy peat fibres are drying up. Always water until the water flows from the bottom of the pot to make sure all the soil is moistened. If you've let it get bone dry, you may have to water it twice. The edibles in this category are mostly herbs, such as rosemary and thyme, that come from hot countries where poor, sandy or even rocky soil is the norm.

Cucumbers need consistent moisture.

These are the plants that like their moisture level just right. I still recommend a freely-draining medium and an empty saucer (or none at all) underneath. When the surface begins to dry, poke your finger into the soil. If it's dry to the first knuckle, it's time to water. Many of the most famous edibles, including tomatoes and cucumbers, fall into this category. They tend to get bitter if they are allowed to wilt between waterings.

These are often tropical or marginal plants, and they need to be kept consistently moist. When the surface of the soil is beginning to dry out, water it again. If you want to take an extra step to ensure their health, put a layer of cedar mulch on the soil in your container. Mulch isn't just for perennial and shrub beds; in a container it prevents evaporation and looks and smells wonderful. Several edible varieties from low-lying tropical areas, like watercress, need steady moisture.

Just because a plant needs a lot of water does not mean that it can be planted in muddy soil that doesn't drain very well, or in a pot with no holes. Lots of water doesn't mean stagnant water. Plant roots pull oxygen out of the water just like fish gills and will deoxygenate stagnant water until the plant drowns in it. I plant all of my plants, no matter their moisture requirements, in the same well-draining medium; the difference is in the amount I water.

## Question #3: Accessibility

While vegetable gardening is probably the most established style of gardening we have in Canada, growing edibles in mixed containers is just starting to gain mainstream popularity. The confluence of very old and very new styles has led to a wide gap in what is available. When you're shopping for edible plants, you'll notice that some varieties, such as oregano and tomatoes, can be found almost anywhere, while varieties such as shiso and figs can be exasperatingly hard to track down. This obstacle is one that any gardener can easily leap over with the help of some key technological tools.

It's always frustrating to read about an exciting ingredient, whether it's in a gardening book or a cookbook, and not be able to get your hands on it.

For this book, I've made sure that, as of the time of writing, all the edible plants here can be found either by calling around to garden centres or with a quick internet search.

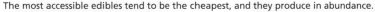 You'll be able to find these plants in almost any Canadian town or city, often throughout the year. They include the most popular vegetables and classic herbs. Many old-fashioned, seed-grown varieties, like beans, beets and carrots, are also included in this category. If you build a container of these plants, not only will they be easy to find, but they also probably won't cost you very much. These plants aren't exotic, but they tend to be cheap, easy to care for, reliable yielders. If you're growing food because you're on a tight budget, look for the little feet.

The most accessible edibles tend to be the cheapest, and they produce in abundance.

 While these plants probably aren't available at your local box store, if you live in or near a large city you shouldn't have any issues finding them. Get on the phone to the independent garden centres around you and ask about availability, size and price of what you're looking for. Keep in mind that smaller independents have often built up niche markets of plants such as heirloom tomatoes, and if you're willing to search, you might find great value.

When I wrote *Gardening with Colour*, I made an effort not to include plants that can't be found in a good-sized Canadian city. With this book I knew from day one that I had to break that rule. The varieties of edibles available online today are so vast and so exciting that I just had to include some of them. With a click of the mouse, companies such as Richter's Herbs will ship you plants and seeds that, before the age of the internet, were unheard of in Canadian gardens. Be adventurous and order that plant online; you might just discover the key ingredient to a new favourite dish.

For most hard-to-find edibles, a simple internet search will point the way. Before you buy, I suggest browsing online reviews of the supplier (simply type their name along with "reviews" into Google) to make sure they're reputable. Stick to Canadian suppliers unless you want to wade through a maze of red tape.

You may have to order red shiso from an online supplier, like Richters Herbs.

## Question #4: Complexity

This is the "how easy is it to grow?" query that accompanies many edibles bought by beginner gardeners. I use the term "complexity" because I believe that no plant is actually difficult to grow. The most complex varieties simply require more steps, like pruning, overwintering or physical support, and may be finicky about watering. Even beginners can grow them if they check in on them more often.

This book is about educating and inspiring, so the last thing I want to do is scare anyone off of growing. While I'm not going to write a book full of plants that make people drool but are too fiendishly complex to work, I'm also going to be honest with you about what a plant requires to thrive. If you're very unsure about gardening and just starting out, I don't want you to be discouraged with plants that don't work out for you. The confidence you build by harvesting off your patio is what will make you more creative and bold the next year and the next. Start with "green circle" plants if you think you have two black thumbs. My prediction is that, next spring, you'll be back and wanting to have a go at "blue square" plants to expand your repertoire. The most important thing with whatever plants you choose is that you challenge yourself enough to have fun but not so much that you cut into the fruits of your labour.

Some plants require physical support to grow their best.

I struggled with how to represent the complexity of growing in easy to understand symbols. My editor, Sheila Quinlan, suggested using alpine ski symbols, a notion that made me want to head into the mountains this winter!

On the ski hill, these are wide open, groomed runs that pretty much anyone can master. In edible gardening, these plants are a straightforward ride all the way to harvest. Throw the seed in the container, watch it grow (watering occasionally) and enjoy. These plants take minimal care and attention. They typically don't need to be pruned, staked or supported and don't require a lot of fertilizer.

On the ski hill, these groomed slopes, which are slightly steeper than the greens and thus require more awareness, form the majority of overall runs. The same goes with edibles. These plants aren't as hands off as bush beans, but beginners can still easily grow them. You may need to provide a trellis, make sure they're pruned, or make sure they always have water. You won't need to worry about having any gardening skills that are beyond basic.

These runs are steeper than blues and sometimes ungroomed. Although they look scary on the sign, remember that the most frightening part is usually standing at the top of the run looking down; once you get going you usually find your groove. It's the same with edible plants. These varieties have aspects to their growth that will challenge you a little, but there are no cliffs or insurmountable obstacles. From olives, which have unique overwintering needs, to garlic that needs to be planted the fall before you plant the rest of the container, to artichokes that will grow 1.5 m tall, these varieties present puzzles that you will need to work through in order to enjoy the literal fruits of your labours.

Don't be afraid to try growing artichokes.

## Pros and Cons of Growing in Containers

Mixing different types of edibles in containers will be new to a lot of people, and while there are scores of benefits to doing so, there are also some things to remember. Every new method requires us to slightly alter our regular habits. Edible containers are the most exciting thing that has happened to gardening in a long time, but frustrations can emerge if we aren't honest with ourselves about the potential obstacles we'll need to overcome.

### *Redefining Space and Time*

For the first time in history, more people in the world now live in cities than in the countryside. In cities across Canada, millions of people have either a very small yard or a balcony. "Food deserts," which are residential areas where people have very limited access to fresh produce, are becoming alarmingly common in larger centres; corner-store supermarkets die out and people think that, without a plot of land or a car, fresh food can't be a regular part of their lives.

Container gardening allows anyone with a few square feet of sunlight to grow fresh, healthy food. It's a fundamental shift in not only how we grow food, but also where we grow food. Pots are portable and can go anywhere. Their ability to maintain a higher

This stunning edible container at the Teahouse in Stanley Park shows how restaurants are getting on board with edible container gardening as well.

Trimming herbs will help with air circulation and add to the dinner table.

concentration of plants per square foot than ground plots makes them tremendously space efficient. Gardeners can also position them to make the most of whatever sunlight they get by placing heat lovers in the full sun and huddling cool-weather crops in their shade.

The catch to planting edibles close together is that you'll need to keep an eye on what is happening at soil level. As the plants grow, the lower leaves will inevitably crowd each other, constricting air flow and trapping moisture. They're also the natural catch-all for everything that falls from above to rot. Lower leaves are more likely to develop fungal issues as the container matures. You can prevent this by choosing vertical varieties that don't take up much room at soil level, like trellised vines or standard form

plants. Trimming out lower leaves will also help keep the air flowing below.

Growing in pots will change how you interact with your garden. Ground plots require big blocks of maintenance time in order to thrive. We need to commit to blocks of an hour or more to plow, plant, weed and harvest. If you put some edible containers on your patio, you won't notice the time you spend on them because it will be refreshingly spread out. Every day you'll be checking on them, watering, snipping a branch and just plain fussing—but only for a few minutes. When the first red tomato or runner bean appears, it will be a triumph. Container growing isn't about a massive September harvest. It's about harvesting a little and harvesting often, so that every night there can be something home-grown on your plate.

## Watering

You'll probably notice that the biggest difference between regular maintenance for your in-ground vegetable plot and your edible containers is watering. While plants rooted in the ground have access to deep moisture that takes a long time to evaporate, pot-bound roots must do what they can with a fraction of the water. This puts watering in both the pro and the con category. When soil dries out faster it means both that you need to water more and that the plant is growing faster; it's a glass-half-empty or glass-half-full scenario. Plants are 80–90 percent water, and their fruit is usually even more than that. In order to keep a 1.5 m tall tomato plant yielding plump, firm fruit, it will need about a gallon of water per day. While having to water containers more is unavoidable, there are several tricks that gardeners have been using for years to make it easier.

There are a few ways to help keep the soil cool and slow down evaporation. In containers, soil dries faster because there tend to be more colonizing roots (the plants tend to be closer together than in the ground) and it dries from the warm sides of the pot as well as the surface. The more porous the container is, the faster it will lose water. Plastic pots retain water better than clay. Dark coloured pots and metal pots heat up faster, which is an advantage for heat-loving plants, but choose light colours in warmer regions if you want less watering. In heat waves you can also shade your container or water it down to cool it as you water the plant.

Many popular edible varieties, such as tomatoes, cucumbers and peppers, are from tropical regions where they

Plastic pots retain water better than clay.

enjoy both heat and steady moisture. Because they rarely have to dig for moisture like dry-climate plants, they have surface-based roots that are more vulnerable to damage when the soil surface dries. Drying these types out to the point of wilting can quickly lead to small, bitter or even aborted fruit. Spread some organic mulch across the soil surface to keep it moist. Avoid rock, clay shards or anything that heats up in the sun. Choose a natural product, like straw or untreated wood chips, and avoid mulches with chemicals that might leech into the soil, like died mulch and rubber.

The best way to both cut back on watering and ensure a good crop is to plant in a self-watering container. Watering a traditional container gives the plant a very unstable source of water, with abundant amounts at the time of watering and less and less until, hopefully, it gets water again before stress sets in. Self-watering pots have a reservoir at the bottom that stores

water and provides a stable, steady supply to the plant's roots, which wick it upward as needed. Watering from below also avoids water and mud splashing onto cucumber and tomato leaves, which can quickly result in fungal disease.

Self-watering containers have only been widely available in the last few years; their rise in popularity has gone hand-in-hand with edible container gardening. They started as an expensive novelty and, though more affordable lines are becoming more widely available, they are still more expensive to buy than to make at home. If you're more interested in what's in the container than what the container looks like, consider following the surprisingly easy design provided by Laura Peters in Lone Pine's *Small Space Gardening for Canada*. Peters illustrates how to make a self-watering container out of two five-gallon buckets, some PVC pipe and a saw.

Self-watering containers save time and give plants a steady source of water.

## Speed of Growth

The Canadian climate is famous for being incompatible with growing many types of vegetables and, especially, fruits. A lot of work, energy and nutrients go into making an ear of corn, a bunch of grapes or a giant pumpkin, and plants need time to do it right. Unfortunately, our Canadian growing season often doesn't have the time to give.

Canadian gardeners have been planting heat lovers such as tomatoes and peppers in pots for decades, knowing that growing in containers helps speed up the process in a few ways. Fibrous roots grow faster in soil that's warmer and more porous than the ground, and keeping their sensitive roots out of our cold spring ground adds weeks to the growing season. As the summer advances, the radiant heat from the sun hitting the sides of the container continues to warm the roots, keeping the soil in the pot consistently warmer than the ground would be.

Growing plants faster means having to water more frequently and keep a closer eye on their growth, especially if you have numerous varieties in the same pot. A container garden is like a fish tank, and the sharks (more aggressive plants) will try to gobble up the goldfish (passive plants) any chance they get. Keep the pruners handy to cut vines and tendrils off any plants taking over.

## Overwintering Edibles in Containers

As edible container gardening becomes more mainstream and Canadians begin to broaden the ingredients and techniques they use, overwintering is becoming the elephant in the garden. It's not a topic that you'll see discussed much in gardening books because most of them are written with an American reader in mind, and it's not really an issue down south.

Growing plants in raised beds is a great way to speed up their growth and extend the growing season.

As you grow more and more food in containers, you're going to want to broaden your scope of varieties. This will quickly lead you to plants that perform better over multiple seasons, like raspberries and bananas. Even if plants are hardy in your zone, it's not always feasible to leave them in exposed containers through winter. Ground soil insulates roots so that, even as the leaves die back, the submerged portion remains near 0° C. The sides of containers expose roots to lateral freezing, and the roots can quickly get fatally chilled. The key to successfully overwintering edibles in containers is to insulate the sides of the containers from winter's killing touch.

Before you plan on overwintering, check the plant's zone. The more tender the plant is, the more effort you'll need to put in to overwinter it. If the plant is a zone or two lower than your own (e.g., a zone 3 plant in zone 5 Ontario or BC), it should survive with minimal effort on your part. If you want to overwinter a zone 5 blackberry on the zone 3 Prairies, you'll be facing more of a challenge. You may need to move the plant into an unheated shed or garage. Dormant plants don't need significant sunlight, but you'll have to water enough that the soil isn't bone dry. Most garden centres indicate each plant's zone on a tag or sign; if they don't, make sure to ask. If you don't know your zone, look it up online or ask a fellow gardener.

The bigger the pot, the better it is for overwintering. With bigger pots, the roots aren't pressed against the sides as much, so they are better insulated. If you're planning to overwinter a plant, try to position it in the centre of the container and plant the single-season plants around it. You want as much soil between its roots and the container wall as possible.

If you have a yard (or you know someone who does), the best option is to dig a hole and submerge the pot.

These specimen rosemary topiaries at Rideau Hall demonstrate how striking some herbs become when brought inside over the winter months.

Cover it generously with mulch and water it well just before the ground freezes. Try to avoid leaves as mulch; they are an invitation for mice. If you don't have a yard, or you don't want to fill it with holes, wrap Styrofoam, bubble-wrap, burlap or any other insulating material securely around the pot—the thicker the better. Position the pot in a sheltered area, preferably near the house and out of the wind.

If you live in a high-rise where both exposure and wind are issues, don't despair. A thick layer of insulation will block a surprising amount of wind. Covering the sides will also prevent the roots from heating up on freakishly warm February days, which could prematurely wake up the plants and cause serious damage. Once they're sleeping, you want them to stay sleeping until spring.

I spoke to Alison Beck, avid horticulturalist and garden writer, about some overwintering tips. For balconies, she suggested putting the pot in a cardboard box and filling the empty spaces with soil or packed newspaper. For gardeners with a yard, Alison suggested another trick: "Window wells are an ideal place to overwinter pots. Window wells are a hole that has already been dug. There will always be some heat lost from the basement from the window glass, especially in older houses." Fill in the hole with mulch; bark or straw works well or, if you have mouse problems, consider using Styrofoam packing peanuts or packed snow.

Plants like blackberries and garlic require overwintering in order to yield. Others, like perennial artichokes and raspberries, provide better yields once they're older. Don't be afraid to overwinter pots. It only sounds intimidating because it's rarely discussed and somewhat mysterious. As edible container gardening continues to mature, overwintering will become a normal part of keeping a diverse edible garden.

Raspberries do better over multiple seasons, so don't be afraid to try overwintering.

## Bringing Plants Indoors

I've included several plants that are much more expensive and harder to find than the average Canadian

If you're tired of not getting anything from your houseplants, try a fig. Put it in a sunny indoor spot in winters and in summers it will reward you with successively larger crops.

edible. Although the majority of your edible garden will likely be staple beans, tomatoes and rosemary, I invite you to be adventurous with a few plants and try a multi-year specimen or two.

Centrepiece edibles such as olives, figs and bananas aren't cheap, but from a design perspective they will provide a powerful focal point that will bring a sense of scale to the green shapelessness that tends to characterize edible gardens. If you do take the time to find one, remember that you're buying it for a lot more than one summer.

The big specimen plants will need to come inside every winter, as many of them will take several years to yield. You can also bring many smaller plants indoors in fall only to enjoy a larger crop the next season. Almost anything tropical, from peppers to lemon grass to basil, will thrive indoors.

Plants don't tend to take up as much space in your home as you think they will. Find the sunniest window, preferably tucked out of the way as they often aren't pretty in winter, and water occasionally to keep them from drying out. Depending on how cold tolerant they are and how intense your sunlight is, you may need to wait until well after the last frost and/or acclimatize them slowly to the afternoon sun before moving them back outside in spring. The reward will be well worth the extra effort.

## Transplanting

Growing edibles in mixed container gardens inevitably involves transplanting. This is a double-edged sword because even though your new container is larger and more accommodating, you can easily damage the root system and, by extension, reduce the yield.

To transplant, turn your plant upside down and gently squeeze the pot around the rootball to loosen it until it slips out on its own. Never grab the stem and yank as if you're pulling a carrot. Many of the edibles we use, like tomatoes, peppers and cucumbers, are tropical plants with very delicate, surface-based root systems, and one good yank is all they need to shut down production for the year.

I'm not a big fan of cutting the rootball open like a cake. This method works for root-bound annuals and shrubs, but edibles tend to be more delicate. If the plant is root-bound, massage the roots gently to loosen them before planting it in your new container.

If you're too rough in your transplanting, either by yanking on the stem or by jamming the rootball into a space that's too small for it, the plant will remind you of it later. Curled parsley will bolt, pepper flowers and fruit will abort, and cucumbers, if treated too roughly, will die.

Beans, carrots, peas, beets, parsnips, nasturtiums, salad greens and even some herbs never need to be transplanted. Drop the seed on the soil surface where you want the plant to be, sprinkle some soil on top of it, water and walk away. You may think it will take a long time to grow something from seed, but if you plant a bean seed side by side with an established starter plant, the seed gets to 60 cm tall in the time it takes the starter plant to recover from the shock of being transplanted.

Transplanting isn't all bad. It gives you the chance to apply supplements right to the roots where they will be most efficient. Bone meal and Myke (a mycorrhizae-based supplement that increases yields) are excellent additions. If you're planting tomatoes or peppers, especially if it's into an acidic peat moss-based medium, add some lime or eggshells for calcium. Calcium will help prevent those rotted patches at the base of the fruit, otherwise known as blossom end-rot.

It's good to get an indoor headstart on tomato seedlings, but take care not to plant them so early that they stretch owing to lack of light.

## Designing with Edibles

Now for the really exciting part. For decades, Canadian gardeners have grown and cherished their vegetable gardens in the obscurity of their backyards. While geraniums and petunias bloomed and flourished on the front step, tomatoes and carrots were kept out of sight behind the fence; rows of beans and broccoli were considered best used and not seen.

I have the happy privilege of telling people that times have changed, and the days of keeping edibles in the closet are over. With the explosion in popularity of using vegetables

This planter at Minter Gardens, overflowing with 'Triple Curled' parsley, shows just how striking this soft-spoken herb can be.

and fruits in containers, people are rethinking the old stereotype that edibles are ugly. We seem wired to think that, just because something is useful, it can't also be beautiful. Annuals, whose only use is beauty, take the spotlight while we often don't even think of edibles in that way. To use a pop-culture analogy, it's like we've only ever thought of edibles as a friend, but now it's time to start thinking of them as something "more."

In this book, I'll make you a believer that containers full of edibles can be beautiful enough to sit proudly on any front step, porch or patio in Canada. It's an exciting time in gardening because not only can you stop keeping your edible plants hidden, but you can also display them proudly knowing that planting a pot full of strawberries and beets puts you on the cutting edge of Canadian gardening innovation. In my last book, *Gardening with Colour*, I spent a lot of time discussing how to use the elements of design in your container gardens. Although that book was focused on annuals and this book is about edibles, you can use the same principles to make your containers look fabulous.

The first step toward making your pots of veggies beautiful is to realize that they contribute much more to your yard than just food. We've grown accustomed to looking at annuals as aesthetic objects and edibles as objects of utility. While designing with annuals seems very natural, edibles, as utilitarian plants, often seem to have no aesthetic worth. The truth is that edibles can be gorgeous enough to give annuals a run for their money, but we need to think a little differently about how to design with them than we're used to.

The elements of design are the basic building blocks of art. There are about seven or eight of them, but I'll only be discussing the ones that are directly relatable to you as a gardener.

Some of the elements, like line, aren't as applicable to container gardening as others. The following are the elements that I will consistently refer to throughout the book as they come up.

## Colour

When talking about annuals, the focus invariably turns to colour. Over the last few decades annuals have been bred to have more vivid and abundant flowers than ever before. This has turned annuals into the natural champions of container gardening while making edibles seem all the more, well, green.

Swiss chard creates a stunning central feature in this long promenade garden at the Montreal Botanical Garden.

New, high-octane varieties of annuals have made us accustomed to containers that boast a bewildering amount of colour. Colour has become such a dominant element of design in container gardening that we think less about the others. We need to get out of the "colour is king" mentality with edibles. While bright red peppers, splotched radicchio leaves and purple sage bring some

Embrace the potential of green in edible design.

variety, edible pots are, inevitably, going to be omni-presently green.

To design with edibles, we need to fall back in love with green. Luckily, green is one of the richest and most complex colours in the spectrum. Green is the colour of life and rebirth, and I believe that we have a deeper, more innate love for green than any other colour.

We often take green for granted. It is the anchoring colour in the garden, its potential often dismissed as background noise like music in an elevator. But there is so much more to green than the colour of your lawn. Designs with nothing but greens can easily be some of most beautiful, albeit complex, in the garden.

Green isn't as passive in the garden as many people think. In containers with hot, bold, red tomatoes or peppers, the green will balance the intense colour like holding back a wild animal. The soft, emerald greens of basil, nasturtiums and lettuce bring thoughts of fresh and vibrant new life, while the dark, lush greens of rosemary and tomato leaves inspire meditative thoughts of nurturing and deep growth. Every garden has green in it; the key is to remember that it plays as active a role as the other colours around it. It is the colour we see most often but also in many ways the most difficult to use in design because it is so nuanced and has so many faces.

## Texture

As a boy, I would look at pictures of Van Gogh's "Starry Night" and Monet's "Water-lilies" and think they were pretty, but I didn't understand what the big deal was. As a man, travelling to Paris to see the master-works in person, it was like I was seeing them for the first time. Staring at the way Van Gogh used texture, globbing and mashing and smearing the oil across the canvas (my nose probably closer to it than it should have been), I fell in love with the texture of the pieces. It was tantalizing and I wanted to touch those stars and those water-lilies to experience that texture.

In gardening, texture is one of the most underappreciated and important elements. While colour gets the spotlight and most of our attention, there is just as much "wow" factor and number of options in texture as there are in colour. And unlike in the museum, in the garden there are no "Do Not Touch" signs.

Texture is as visual as it is tactile. When you look at soft sages or glossy citrus leaves, your mind tells you how they're going to feel even before you touch them. A variety of textures in the garden invigorates the tactile imagination and makes a garden come to life. While colour excites only the eyes, texture adds another dimension as you anticipate how a plant will feel as well as enjoy the way it looks.

When you're choosing your edibles, keep their textures in the back of your mind. Think of texture as the third dimension of the garden. Colour is the second dimension, the eye candy that no garden should be without. Texture is usually less showy but can often be more dynamic.

Use texture to make people want to touch as well as look.

## Form and Shape

In container gardening, the form is what the composition as a whole looks like when all the ingredients are

Use a myriad of shapes to create an interesting form.

planted together. In gardening, unlike sculpture, the form changes as the plants grow and compete, making form a dynamic and exciting element. Form is the overall composition, but within that form the individual plants all relate to each other via the principles of design. Shape refers to the shapes of the plants making up the design. Form is the forest; shape is the trees. A myriad of shapes, whether they are leaves, flowers, stems or anything else within the composition, all play against each other to create the grand form.

The shapes of the plants can be used to create contrast and harmony and make the overall form dynamic. Harmonious shapes are similar to each other; they might have similar leaf shapes or growing habits that bind them together into a pattern that the eye can grab onto. If the shapes within the container are alike and harmonious, then the overall form will have a calming sense of unity that makes it pleasing to look at. But if the shapes are contrasting (e.g., different leaf shapes), then the container will have an extra layer of dynamism to excite the eye. Onions, chives and even rosemary have harmonious shapes. Throw some basil in there for contrast and you'll make it more stimulating to look at. As with colour and texture, too much harmony will cause your creations to become so unified that they will stop being exciting to look at, whereas too much contrast will have the eye craving a sense of pattern and unity.

Without a mass of colourful flowers at their disposal, edible container gardeners need to take a closer look at how the shapes and forms of their plants and containers complement each other. Container gardens are living compositions, and the first thing the eye notices when it looks at them is the overall form of how the plants grow together. A single plant in a container is like a lyric in a song or a fraction of a painted canvas; while it may be beautiful in itself, how it blends with the other elements is what will bring the whole composition alive.

There are a lot of shapeless edibles out there that, while delicious on the dinner plate, aren't very inspiring to look at (I'm talking about you, bush beans). Inevitably, shapeless herbs and veggies will be staples of your designs; to give them a pleasing form, you'll need to seek out eye-catching shapes where you can. Trellises, tall elements such as corn and architectural elements such as rosemary and yucca will bring much-needed diversity to your living sculpture.

To garden is to create living art that changes its form as it grows throughout the season, which makes it both challenging and exciting. If you spent a lot of time and energy planning an exact and precise form, you may be disappointed in a month or two, especially if you planted aggressive plants with passive plants. If the various plants in the container aren't compatible with each other, one will become dominant over the others, which will change the balance of the composition. It can be very exciting to watch your work of art grow and change as the months roll by, even though sometimes the form will change in ways you didn't expect.

Give nasturtiums something to climb, and they will become a living sculpture.

## Designing with Food

You'll notice that many of the container recipes in this book have a lot to do with culinary recipes. When designing with edibles there's more to think about than blending colour, texture and form. It's food, and as we choose the plants to use we're also choosing our menu for the months ahead. The edible dimension is another thing to think about as we're planning our pots; on top of making them look beautiful, we also want to use edibles that we want to eat. You may love fennel's lacy texture, but if you don't want to eat fennel, there probably isn't much point planting it.

I had a lot of fun designing these containers and growing them in my "workshop" at Salisbury Greenhouse. Except for a few recipes that are devoted solely to exploring colour, all the containers have a culinary or useful herbal theme to them. Unlike annual containers, where I have access to a bewildering array of

Find the balance between what looks great in a container and what you want on your plate, because these two things don't always go together.

options, these recipes were so specific that I had very little flexibility in my options. Nevertheless, the results show that you can create beautiful containers even while working within a recipe, like ingredients for salsa, or even a regional theme, as in using only Vietnamese ingredients.

## Caution

Different people metabolize foods differently and have different sensitivities. Every time we introduce a new food into our systems, there is the chance of an allergic reaction.

I'm going to present you with a host of new edibles, and I hope to make you hungry to try them. I suggest trying new foods one at a time so that, if you do have an allergic reaction, you'll be able to identify what the culprit is right away. Some of these plants, like gogi berries, need several levels of preparation in order to eat them. Many of them have parts that aren't edible. I've tried to leave out plants that have toxic parts to them, like alocasia, but nevertheless I caution that unless you know how to prepare these foods, don't eat them. Varieties like scarlet runner bean may look like they are edible right off the vine, but they aren't.

If you are pregnant, breastfeeding or even trying to get pregnant, please approach the medicinal herbs in this book with caution. Like all medicines,

herbs contain very powerful chemicals and they need to be taken responsibly. I've tried to not include any of the more volatile herbs here, but you should still chat with your doctor before starting any herbal medicinal program to make sure that it doesn't conflict with your current condition.

Goji berries have astronomical antioxidants, but traditionally they are dried and cooked before they're eaten.

# FIESTA
## Ingredients for Mexican Cuisine

**Height:** to 2 m

**MEXICAN FOOD IS FAMOUS** for being colourful and full of feisty, fiery flavours. To reflect this, I chose a broad array of shapes and tastes to plant up.

Just because we're planting food doesn't mean our containers can't be aesthetically interesting. There are a number of architectural elements here, from yucca to corn to a trellis, which bring some much needed symmetry to the shapeless clumps of watercress and oregano. Edible architectural plants are few and far between, so take advantage of any opportunity to use one or three of them.

A  Yucca

B  Rosemary 'Tuscan Blue'

C  Agave 'Boudin Blue'

D  Spearmint

E  Anise-hyssop

F  Mexican oregano

G  Corn 'Northern Super Sweet'

H  Pinto beans

I  Habanero pepper

J  Jalapeno pepper 'Mucho Nacho'

K  Tomatillo

L  Basil

M  Watercress

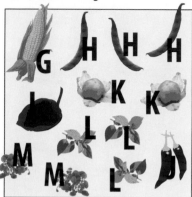

**Recommended container size:** 50 cm by 50 cm / 60 cm by 60 cm

---

From a design perspective, these containers show just how dynamic edible mixes can be. Besides the green bushy elements that we expect to find, there is towering corn, architectural agave, hovering tomatillos and a dramatic trellis. The aesthetics of edibles are based more on shape and texture than on colour, but there is as much potential for beautiful designs with these plants as there is with annuals.

I've planted my Mexican edibles in some old metal washing basins. When using antiques, I recommend lining the containers with clear plastic (with drainage holes) to prevent unwanted chemicals from leeching into the edibles.

In the sun, the metal heats the roots and will quickly dry out the soil on the edges. While the warmth is ideal for growing heat lovers like agave, peppers and corn, make sure to keep an eye on your containers and have the watering can at the ready. If you find that the soil in your container is drying out too quickly, consider shading the container so it doesn't get the direct sun, keeping in mind that this will slow down the growth.

Yucca makes a vividly architectural centrepiece, like in this container at the Toronto Botanical Garden.

Mexican cooking uses a wide array of plants with many different growing conditions. I've planted the dry-loving edibles (yucca, agave, oregano) in one container and the edibles that don't like to dry out (peppers, watercress) in the other. This makes it far easier to control their different watering needs than it would be if they were all in the same pot.

Depending on where you are, the larger plants in these containers will take most or all of the growing season to produce. Corn, pinto beans, tomatillos, agaves and yucca are all long-season plants. Start with large starter plants and put them in the hottest spot you can. The metal pots will slightly shorten the maturity times, but in colder regions (e.g., the Prairies) it will be tight. Once you find some agave and yucca fruits, bring them inside in fall to use as houseplants.

When it comes to companion planting, beans are beneficial to almost any other plants thanks to their nitrogen-fixing ability. Try not to pair them with the Allium family, however, as Alliums will inhibit beans' growth.

Tomatillos grow into shrubs that will dominate your container, but reward you with scores of fruit in late summer and into fall.

Habaneros are the hottest naturally occurring pepper in the world, and more hybrids come out every year.

## Cooking with these Pots

Mexican cuisine is as diverse as the country and uses foods grown in ecosystems from arid deserts to steaming jungles. Corn, beans, chili peppers and squash are the most obvious Mexican staples. I incorporated the first three but felt that squash, being so massive, was a container too far. I then divided my Mexican recipe into two pots, one arid and one moist, in order to work with the different growing conditions presented by such a diverse country.

While you wait for the longer season crops, you can graze on the herbs and peppers as they ripen. The watercress, basil and mint will grow quickly, so don't be shy about snipping them off to add to your dishes on a regular basis.

This cuisine combination won't provide all the ingredients for any one Mexican dish, but it will be a start for many. The goal is to provide a few homemade edibles for many dishes so that you serve them knowing that you grew the corn for the tortillas, the peppers for the fajitas and the tomatillos for the salsa.

Choose an early-maturing variety of corn (look for the number on the seed pack or tag) for better odds of a bountiful harvest.

Pintos are a mottled bean that is essential for authentic Mexican cooking. Serve alongside rice or mashed into refried beans.

## Mayan Technique

In the spring of 2012, I created a "workshop" in the back of Salisbury Greenhouse where I spent many happy, creative afternoons. Teeming with edible plants and full of experimental combinations and techniques, it's where most of the containers in this book were grown.

One day as I worked there, Mario Salazar, our head grower and a native of El Salvador, noticed the Mexican-inspired ingredients I had pulled aside. He told me about an ancient Mayan method of planting known as milpa farming. It's an agricultural model wherein up to a dozen different crops, including beans, corn and squash, are planted together in a small area. Together they create a complementary web: the beans fix nitrogen in the soil and use the corn as a climbing support, and the large squash leaves shade the soil and suppress weeds. The milpa system generates large yields and many people have pointed to it as an alternative to mono-culture, which is the practice of planting vast amounts of one crop and saturating the soil with synthetic nutrients to fulfill its needs.

### A Yucca

*Yucca filamentosa;* Adam's needle

This yucca is identified by the white threads that hang off its fleshy leaves. It's easy to grow as long as it's not overwatered, and you can bring it inside for winter. When it blooms, its creamy white, drooping flowers can tower 3 m in the air. You can eat the flowers raw or dried in salads or as a seasoning; they have a bitter onion taste.

### B Rosemary 'Tuscan Blue'

*Rosmarinus officinalis*

see p. 217

### C Agave 'Boudin Blue'

*Agave attenuata;* foxtail agave

Agave is one of the most famous edible plants of Mexico, largely because of *A. tequilana. A. attenuata* is native to central Mexico and has become a popular garden plant thanks to its lack of sharp spines. Its flowers are delicious when roasted. Make sure to give it well-drained soil. And, unlike some desert plants, it also prefers some loam and organic matter mixed in.

### D Spearmint

*Mentha spicata*

see p. 102

### E Anise-hyssop

*Agastache foeniculum*

Anise-hyssop is a perennial with a sweet anise scent that grows up to 90 cm tall. It thrives in well-drained, even sandy, soil. It will aid in pollination by acting like a bee magnet. Some First Nations used it as a sweetener, and the dried leaves make a delicious licorice-flavoured tea. Add the seeds to baked goods.

### F Mexican oregano

   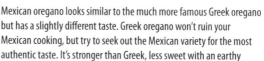

*Lippia graveolens*

Mexican oregano looks similar to the much more famous Greek oregano but has a slightly different taste. Greek oregano won't ruin your Mexican cooking, but try to seek out the Mexican variety for the most authentic taste. It's stronger than Greek, less sweet with an earthy spice. It's perfect for salsa and chili. Add it early in cooking, like a bay leaf, to let its flavour infuse through the dish.

### Ⓖ Corn 'Northern Super Sweet'
*Zea mays*

This is a great variety for Canadians to grow. It's very early (67 days) and yields 23 cm long ears on 1.2–1.8 m tall plants. The corn is very sweet and tastes great cooked on the barbecue or any way you like. Give it as much sun and heat as possible in well-drained soil.

### Ⓗ Pinto beans
*Phaseolus vulgaris*

This bean has played an important role in Mexican cuisine and culture for centuries. Grow it in well-drained soil and harvest the oval-shaped, spotted beans when the pods have dried out. Start it indoors in early spring because it takes longer than the average bean. Cook and serve pinto beans with almost anything, or use them for refried beans.

### Ⓘ Habanero pepper
*Capsicum chinense*

see p. 159

### Ⓙ Jalapeno pepper 'Mucho Nacho'
*Capsicum annuum*

see p. 186

### Ⓚ Tomatillo
*Physalis ixocarpa;* tomato verde

The tomatillo is a Mexican staple. The plants grow to about 90 cm tall, and the cherry-sized fruit ripens inside an inedible papery husk. Pick when the husk is light brown (green is under-ripe and yellow is over-ripe) and smooth. You will need to grow two plants to ensure pollination and fruit set. They are as versatile as tomatoes in cooking.

### Ⓛ Basil
*Ocimum basilicum*

see p. 127

### Ⓜ Watercress
*Nasturtium officinale*

Closely related to nasturtiums and native to Asia Minor, watercress is one of the oldest cultivated plants in human history. It grows so fast that I suggest keeping it in containers. Its hollow stems have a peppery taste that works well in soups, salads and sandwiches.

# ONE NIGHT IN BANGKOK
## Ingredients for Thai Cuisine

**Height:** to 2 m

**CANADIANS HAVE GOTTEN HOOKED** on Thai cooking. From the exotic tensions of flavour to heat that makes you run for the water, dishes like pad thai, tom yam soup and green curry are becoming essential culinary experiences.

Thailand is proudly the only Southeast Asian country that has never been colonized, and the Thai people have developed a unique style of cooking that is influenced more by their local neighbours than by European traditions.

- **A** Banana 'Zebrina'
- **B** Cucumber 'Sweet Slice'
- **C** Broccoli 'Packman'
- **D** Garlic
- **E** Chinese cabbage
- **F** Peas 'Sugar Snap'

- **G** Basil 'Thai'
- **H** Lemon grass
- **I** Chili pepper 'Thai'

- **J** Eggplant 'Amethyst'
- **K** Garlic chives

**Recommended container size:** 45 cm across / 35 cm across / 20 cm across

This simple container features hot Thai peppers and a mix of purple and Thai basil. It would look great on any kitchen windowsill.

Jungles are the perfect model for designing container gardens and the one I usually use. Conjure the image of a towering canopy, lush understorey and shady forest floor and try to keep it in your mind's eye as you design your next container. I modelled these containers to reflect the frenetic layered lushness of the Southeast Asian jungle, which is so thick that walking through it makes you wonder what is lurking just out of sight, watching you. The banana and eggplant form the canopy while the chives, broccoli and cabbage create a thick understorey.

Thai cuisine varies by region, but the climatic conditions across the regions aren't nearly as disparate as in a country like Mexico. All of these edibles love plenty of sun and evenly moist soil with a dash of organic matter (compost, manure, etc.) blended in.

The Chinese cabbage, peas and broccoli prefer life on the cool side, so if you have some protection from the afternoon sun they'd appreciate it. The cucumbers should still perform well; plant them in their own pot next time if they don't.

You can easily train your peas to climb the banana. To do so, leave a few inches of stump when you nip off spent lower leaves (or just leave them on). Pea tendrils need something to climb; they will grab the stumps and sprint toward the canopy.

Although it's not the sexiest of container plants, broccoli is beneficial to any aromatic herb (rosemary, sage, dill, etc.) and most vegetables. Try to keep it away from tomatoes, pole beans and strawberries. Chinese cabbage grows very well alongside other members of the Brassica family, which includes broccoli and cauliflower. Keep it away from corn plants.

If Colorado potato beetle is a problem in your area, be warned that it loves eggplant even more than potatoes. Green beans repel it, so consider seeding some in your eggplant container.

Eggplant flowers look like origami stars made of delicate purple paper. They bring unexpected beauty wherever they go.

'Pot Black' eggplant yields so much ping-pong ball-sized fruit that you may have to stake it so it doesn't tip over.

Thai peppers aren't unbearably hot, but they have a potent kick to them. Try a taste on your tongue before you eat the whole thing.

## Cooking with these Pots

While much of Western cooking celebrates one type of flavour, whether it be sweet, savoury, etc., Thai cooking thrives in the deliberate balance between various different flavours. It's common for a Thai dish to be spicy, sweet, savoury and even sour at the same time.

When you prepare your own Thai-themed container garden, try to keep in mind the kaleidoscope of flavours that the food presents our palates. I blended the sweetness of snap peas and slicing cucumbers and the sharp spice of chilis and garlic with savoury eggplant and Thai basil. Throw them all together with lemon grass and broccoli, and you end up with three containers with as many different flavours as the cooking itself.

There are many levels of harvesting here, from herbs you can harvest almost immediately to bananas that will take years to bear fruit (I included them so you can use the leaves as wraps). I used quickly maturing varieties of eggplant, peas and cucumber so that you can get cooking with them sooner. If you want more authenticity, look for Thai eggplant.

As the chili peppers ripen, the best way to use them is fresh. If you love pain there are hotter varieties available, but use caution, as some ultra hot varieties are actually dangerous. The cucumbers are an effective and traditional way to cool the mouth after a spicy plunge.

## Use Caution

Writing about food, especially types of food that many people haven't tried before, carries a lot of responsibility. As I researched hundreds of varieties of edible plants for this book, that responsibility lingered in the back of my mind. That's why taro isn't included in any of the Asian-inspired combinations.

Taro (*Colocasia esculenta*) has been a staple in Oceanic, Asian and African cultures for thousands of years. The plant's corms (the bulbous roots) are an easily digestible and vitamin-rich starch when cooked. When uncooked, however, the corm is inedible due to calcium oxalate, which must be broken down (as during the cooking process) to be digestible. The leaves and sap of the plant are also toxic. On top of that, other varieties of *Colocasia*, some of which look almost identical, aren't edible at all. Even some hybrids of *Colocasia esculenta*, which tend to be the ornamental types available in garden centres, became inedible when they were hybridized.

*Colocasia* is closely related to, and often confused with, *Alocasia*. *Alocasia*

is another big-leafed beauty that presented the same dilemma. The corms and even the stems of certain species are edible, while parts of other species are toxic and even deadly.

I didn't think it was appropriate to include a plant with toxic twins and that required such careful preparation. If you are interested in trying taro, you can sometimes buy the corms and/or prepared taro in specialty grocery stores.

Unless you know what you're doing, get your colocasia root (taro) from the supermarket and leave the plant in the container.

## Ⓐ Banana 'Zebrina'
*Musa acuminata*

'Zebrina' is a dwarf variety of the Sumatran blood banana, which is named for the red splotches splashed across its leaves. Its seedy fruit is edible but takes a few years to arrive. In the meantime, use its leaves to wrap Asian-inspired dishes, like fish, before cooking. While the leaves themselves are technically edible, they contain a rather chewy fibre that makes them better seen than tasted. Let the suckers that it sends up grow and you'll get a clump of banana rhizomes.

## Ⓑ Cucumber 'Sweet Slice'
*Cucumis sativus*

As long as you have ample direct sunlight and a sturdy trellis, cucumbers basically grow themselves. Slicing cucumbers are sweetest when they're picked right off the vine and eaten fresh, but pick them when they are green and not yellow. They won't get bitter if you keep the soil moist (mulching helps). They can trail over the side of a container, as long as it's tall enough that the fruit doesn't touch the ground.

## Ⓑ Broccoli 'Packman'
*Brassica oleracea* var. *botrytis*

A popular and nutritious vegetable worldwide, broccoli is known for its culinary versatility, nutritional value and tendency to be loathed by children everywhere. 'Packman' is an early variety suited for Canadian seasons. It performs best in cool temperatures, so try to plant it right around the last frost date. 'Packman' is a Calabrese type broccoli (the big flower head) and will grow about 60 cm tall as it produces its stalk.

## Ⓓ Garlic
*Allium sativum*

Savvy gardeners have been growing garlic for 6000 years. Native to Central Asia, it is one of the most useful herbs out there for both cooking and its health benefits. It's easy to grow in the ground but requires overwintering in Canadaian containers. If you have a large pot, start it in fall a few weeks before freeze-up. Plant each clove separately (break up the head), and harvest when the leaves start to die back.

### Ⓔ Chinese cabbage

*Brassica rapa* subsp. *pekinensis*

A classic Asian vegetable, Chinese cabbage prefers the cool temperatures of spring and should be planted right after the last frosts. It doesn't like to be transplanted, so consider direct seeding it. Keep the soil moist to keep the greens tender, and a compact head should form in a couple of months; slice it off at the base to harvest, or eat the leaves at your leisure. Try to keep it away from peppers and okra.

### Ⓕ Peas 'Sugar Snap'

*Pisum sativum*

see p. 225

### Ⓖ Basil 'Thai'

*Ocimum basilicum;* Thai basil, Asian basil

This attractive little plant bears spicy, licorice-flavoured leaves on dark red stems. Harvest by nipping off the tender tips of the stems early in the morning when the flavour is strongest. Never pinch too far down the stem. The late-summer flowers are dark and gorgeous but they will lessen the plant's flavour, so you will have to choose: flavour or beauty.

### Ⓗ Lemon grass

*Cymbopogon citratus*

see p. 71

### Ⓘ Chili pepper 'Thai'

*Capsicum annuum*

see p. 115

### Ⓙ Eggplant 'Amethyst'

*Solanum melongena*

see p. 103

### Ⓚ Garlic chives

*Allium tuberosum;* nira, Oriental garlic

This little plant packs a surprisingly garlicky taste. Popular in Asian dishes such as stir-fries and dumplings, it boasts pretty, edible flowers that you can either keep, eat or snip off. The chives will develop the best flavour in moist soil and should be harvested often by cutting off a few stems. They are perennial and may prove invasive in warmer regions, so keep them pot-bound.

# BON APPETIT
## Ingredients for French Cuisine

**Height:** to 1 m

**FRENCH CUISINE HAS EVOLVED** and adapted over the centuries, but one thing has always remained constant. Great French cooking is the triumph of simple, fresh ingredients either bought that day from the local market or, ideally, grown on your own plot of rolling countryside.

I kept this combination simple as a salute to the simple rural roots of French food. All the herbs and vegetables here would be very much at home among the grapevines of the Loire, the lavender of Normandy or the sunflowers of Provence.

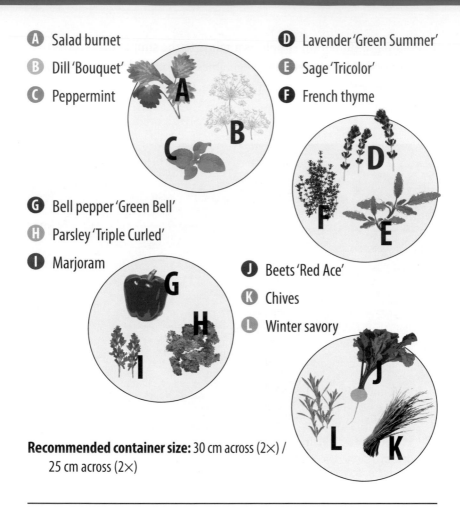

**A** Salad burnet

**B** Dill 'Bouquet'

**C** Peppermint

**D** Lavender 'Green Summer'

**E** Sage 'Tricolor'

**F** French thyme

**G** Bell pepper 'Green Bell'

**H** Parsley 'Triple Curled'

**I** Marjoram

**J** Beets 'Red Ace'

**K** Chives

**L** Winter savory

**Recommended container size:** 30 cm across (2×) / 25 cm across (2×)

This combination used a very simple design tactic that I replicated in the four pots. Taking advantage of the way our eye naturally moves in a clockwise direction across objects, I made the four to mirror each other. Each of these containers has three sizes of elements, and they all go from biggest to smallest in a clockwise direction. Our eyes will move from big to small in the same direction around all of them, visually grouping them together. You can use this technique in your spring container, your garden design and almost anything else.

I chose terracotta pots because they are ubiquitous in France and conjure a sense of Old World nostalgia that no other material can match. If you live in a dry region of Canada, be aware that terracotta is porous. Dry air will wick water from the pot, and the pot will in turn wick water from the roots, drying them out. Keep the water-wand handy or choose another material.

Although lavender isn't culinary, no French combination should be without it. Besides being beloved for its nostalgic presence in potpourris and sachets, lavender repels an assortment of unwelcome creatures, including ticks, mice and moths. Savvy gardeners sometimes use bundles of lavender in infested areas.

You may need to keep your eye on the peppermint, parsley and lavender so that they don't bully their buddies. Luckily these three herbs are among the most versatile, so it's not hard to find an excuse to snip them.

The dill is going to get large, so don't be afraid of harvesting the leaves if you don't want to wait for the seeds. Chopped dill brings its trademark aroma and taste to everything from salads to fish.

Harvest the peppers as they ripen and the beets when you can't resist them anymore. My beets never make it past the sweet baby stage. Sprinkle more beet seed a few weeks before you harvest so that they germinate and get a head start on another crop.

This herb pot from Plant World in Toronto features marjoram, rosemary, sorrel, tarragon, thyme, French parsely, bay, chervil and chives.

The Montreal Botanical Garden created a living wall of herbs in their outdoor café, and I wasn't able to take my eyes off it.

The beauty of herbs comes from their lush foliage, crisp shapes and the rich green colour that exudes life and vitality.

## Cooking with these Pots

With something as vast as French cooking, which is both complex and highly regional, you will have to assume a very narrow scope of what

If you're weary of red, beets are available in a host of colours to add flair to salads, like 'Jewel Toned Mix' from Renee's Garden.

to plant. I went the rural, provincial, checkered curtain rustling over a windowsill approach.

French cooking is famous for its poultry and sauces, but because you can't grow a plump duck or fresh cream in a pot, I opted for many of the ingredients for *herbs de Provence*, a combination of dried herbs that includes thyme, sage, marjoram, savory and lavender (add basil and rosemary to complete it). It's a classic rub for any meat or to infuse into olive oil.

These pots are ideal for harvesting a little and harvesting often. Herbs are always ripe, so make sure to keep these pots handy so that you can snip off a sprig whenever the occasion calls.

## Using Lavender

I included the Spanish *L. stoechas* in my combination instead of the more classically French *L. dentata* because it's showier in containers and is slightly more versatile in use. Large garden centres will typically have English (*L. angustifolia*) or Spanish to choose from, but the French is out there if you're willing to look for it.

Lavender is one of those plants that people love but often don't know what to do with. I included it here because, although rarely used in traditional French cuisine, it has been an important part of domestic culture there for centuries.

Lavender rewards you with flushes of graceful, paper thin, soft purple flowers.

One of the best things about lavender is its earthy, stabilizing scent. The buds contain the famous essential oil, which you can find infused into pretty much anything. When added to baths, dripped on pillows or allowed to waft through the home, it helps relieve stress, lessen headache pain and relieve anxiety-induced insomnia. If you have a fireplace you can burn some stems. You can also add sachets of buds and essential oil to the dryer to infuse into your clothes or simply hang clusters of it around your home.

This simple container from Proven Winners can help transform your backyard into a cottage garden.

###  Salad burnet
*Sanguisorba minor*

These ferny leaves have a crisp cucumber taste that is used extensively in French cooking. Give it plenty of water in well-drained, nutrient-rich soil. Use the leaves externally to treat minor burns, scalds and sores or add them fresh to salads and enjoy.

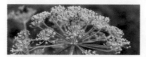

### B Dill 'Bouquet'
*Anethum graveolens*

see p. 103

### C Peppermint
*Mentha* x *piperita*

With a wide range of culinary and medicinal uses, it's understandable why we've been using peppermint for thousands of years. It thrives in woodland conditions: a little shade with moist, organically rich soil. Use its young leaves and flowers to add a crisp flavour to tea or desserts. Thanks to its high menthol content it's an ancient breath freshener. It will also help keep ants and other pests out of your container.

### D Lavender 'Green Summer'
*Lavandula stoechas;* Spanish lavender

Although it has limited culinary uses, the world adores lavender for its medicinal and aromatic uses (it's the best for potpourri). *L. stoechas* is traditionally a Spanish lavender, though it may be labelled as French (which is the harder to find *L. dentata*). It's somewhat drought tolerant, so don't keep it too wet. It also prefers drier air than other varieties, so it's the best choice for Prairie gardeners. Lavender attracts bees and butterflies.

### E Sage 'Tricolor'
*Salvia officinalis;* garden sage

Common sage is easy to grow and tough once it gets established. The irresistibly touchable leaves have a slightly peppery flavour and are best cooked before being eaten. Snip off the flavourful new growth to use with poultry, pork or anything else you fancy. 'Tricolor' tastes the same as common sage but adds an extra splash of variegation to containers to liven up the universal green of herb gardens. After a few years you'll notice it start to lose its flavour and get woody.

### F French thyme
*Thymus vulgaris*

Thyme is a classic herb that is very drought tolerant and can grow in poor, shallow soil. Although both French and English thyme are described as *T. vulgaris*, purists argue that French thyme is the true type because it has curled leaves. French thyme has a subtler taste than English thyme. It is used as a versatile flavouring and as a stuffing for meats, soups and poultry. Pinch buds before they flower and make the taste bitter.

### G Bell pepper 'Green Bell'
*Capsicum annuum*

see p. 159

### H Parsley 'Triple Curled'
*Petroselinum crispum*

see p. 171

### I Marjoram
*Origanum majorana*

One of the oldest herbs in culinary use, marjoram is essential for any cook. It's closely related to oregano but has a milder, sweeter taste than its cousin (you can substitute it for oregano in a pinch). Small and delicate, it is very aromatic and makes a mildly stimulating tea or infused bath. Its medicinal properties come from the antiseptic thymol. Marjoram improves the growth and flavour of any edible it is planted with.

### J Beets 'Red Ace'
*Beta vulgaris*

see p. 147

### K Chives
*Allium schoenoprasum*

see p. 171

### L Winter savory
*Satureja montana*

Winter savory is a small, dark green herb that has a stronger, spicier taste than summer savory. It goes well with beans (both in growing and eating) and light meat dishes like poultry. If the flavour of it is too strong, add it early in the cooking process and it will lighten. It's a natural insect repellent, and rubbing a sprig of it onto a bee or wasp sting will bring some relief.

# FLOATING MARKET
## Ingredients for Vietnamese Cuisine

**Height:** to 2 m

**FROM THE INTOXICATING CHINESE** herbs of Hanoi to the banana-wrapped fish of Ho-Chi-Minh city, it's not easy to forget the food of Vietnam. As the western world rediscovers a country overflowing with vibrant cultural colour, we're also realizing how delicious its food really is.

Ranked as one of the healthiest national cuisines in the world,
Vietnamese food favours the simplicity of carefully chosen herbs
and the freshness of lightly cooked vegetables. A container filled with
Vietnamese ingredients is a tribute to a uniquely Asian taste and
a healthy approach to cooking.

A Vietnamese mint

B Dill 'Bouquet'

C Basil 'Thai'

D Vietnamese coriander

E Rau om

F Fish mint 'Chameleon'

G Red shiso

H Lemon grass

I Banana 'Dwarf Cavendish'

J Watercress

**Recommended container size:**
50 cm across / 35 cm across

The variety of foliage colours, shapes, and textures make this one of my favourite containers of the book.

Vietnamese food is all about freshness, texture and taste. The vegetables have crunch and the herbs have personality. If you're not familiar with these flavours, find some fish mint and Vietnamese coriander to try a leaf before you go online to order your own; the tastes aren't for everybody.

The banana and watercress pot is my salute to the moist Mekong region of southern Vietnam. I'll never forget meandering through floating villages in a boat as old as my grandfather, talking to people about their lives on the water and my first taste of pineapple fresh from a Mekong delta market.

Bananas and watercress like moist soil, but let the surface dry for the banana's sake. If you bring it inside every winter it will grow quite large, but don't be in a hurry to re-pot it. Bananas thrive in the hyper-competitive close quarters of the Asian jungle. The watercress will quickly form a living, peppery mulch over the soil. If you find that the rau om isn't growing well in the other container, bring it to this wetter one.

It will take a few years for the bananas to yield, so don't hold your breath. In the meantime, the leaves make ideal traditional wraps for fish. Bananas are actually rhizomes and when they fruit, the fruiting rhizome will die. Make sure to let the suckers grow freely so you don't trade your plant for a few tiny bananas.

Traditionally wasabi is served on a green shiso leaf, like these grown on the rooftop of the Fairmont Royal York Hotel in Toronto.

Daikon is also known as Chinese radish or Japanese radish and is a favourite for making pickles in Japan and turnip cakes in China.

The Latin name for shiso, a Japanese herb used in Vietnamese cooking, is *Perilla frutescens*. A variegated cultivar, 'Magilla,' is commonly sold in garden centres as an annual. While this is technically shiso, I recommend ordering your own online instead of purchasing an annual with the intention of eating it. While a good garden centre won't use chemicals on their herbs, their annuals are open season. I recommend only eating plants that they have grown knowingly as food.

I included the red shiso because it's more ornamental in a container, but if you want to do more than pickle plums with it, look for the green variety. It may take some calls but it's out there.

## Cooking with these Pots

I relied on unique herbs in this combination because Vietnamese food is famous for exotic flavours coupled with a dedication to fresh, simple ingredients. The best time to harvest herbs is in the morning, but just before cooking is important as well.

These edibles will give you most of the hard-to-find seasonings you'll need for a traditional Vietnamese dish. For example, Thai basil is traditionally served raw alongside the Vietnamese soup pho. For other ingredients, like vegetables and seafood, I suggest finding the nearest Asian supermarket or making a trip to Chinatown.

## Growing Dragonfruit

Tasting fresh dragonfruit (*Hylocereus undatus*) is one of my most vivid memories of Vietnam. I had never tasted anything like it, and the imported dragonfruit I've tried since has had a fraction of the flavour. In Canada, our opportunities to taste fresh, exotic fruit are few and far between. Luckily you can grow dragonfruit, even here!

'Wasabi' arugula from Renee's Garden has a potent, spicy taste and is much easier to grow than wasabi root.

Dragonfruit, also called pitaya, is related to orchid cactus and bears fruit on long, succulent vines that typically need some kind of trellis or support. Even though it needs to have about 10 pounds worth of vines before it yields, it doesn't need a large pot. If the pot looks a little too small for the plant, you have the right size. With their almost non-existent root system, the pot really just acts as a stabilizer.

The flowers, which open only at night, are broad and beautiful. Since Canadian bees only buzz about during the day, you'll have to be the pollinator if you want to make sure you get fruit. Acquire a soft, small paintbrush and, in the middle of the night when the flowers open, spread the pollen from flower to flower.

The author with the dragonfruit plant ordered this summer. It will take a while for fruit, but I'm a patient man.

An easy way to add authenticity to your dishes is to plant Asian eggplant varieties, which are typically long, thin and delicious.

Started plants can be hard to locate but the seed is often easy to find. Either order them online, check with a large garden centre, or try buying a fruit from the grocery store and planting some seeds up. They germinate easily and you should see growth in a day or two. Make sure to dry the plants out between watering; they rot easily with wet feet.

---

### **A** Vietnamese mint

*Mentha x gracilis*

This mint features a spicy spearmint flavour that brings an authentic Vietnamese taste to dishes like salads and pho soup. Like all mints, it's easy to grow and thrives in partial shade with moist soil. Try to pinch flower buds off as you see them. Unlike other mints, keep it away from cold nights. The new group is most flavourful. It's available at Richters herbs.

### **B** Dill 'Bouquet'

*Anethum graveolens*

see p. 103

### **C** Basil 'Thai'

*Ocimum basilicum*

see p. 55

### **D** Vietnamese coriander

*Persicaria odorata*; hot mint

Also called hot mint (though not a mint), this attractively variegated herb adds a spicy twist to salads, beef and stews across Southeast Asia. Traditionally used by Buddhist monks to repress sexual urges, its surprising heat can ruin a dish if there's too much of it; use it in moderation until you get used to it. You may need to keep it pruned so it doesn't take over the container.

### **E** Rau om

*Limnophila aromatica;* rice paddy herb

If your palate is tired of the same old tastes and wants something totally new, boy do I have an herb for you. This heat lover needs to be kept moist and has an aroma somewhere between nutmeg, lemon and curry. Vietnamese and Cambodians use the unique-tasting leaves and stems to flavour soups, meats and spring rolls. It is definitely worth a try and keeps its flavour when dried.

### ⑤ Fish mint 'Chameleon'
*Houttuynia cordata*

Fish mint is one of the more unusual herbs in this book (it is available through Richters), and it comes with a strong fishy smell and taste—it's an acquired taste. 'Chameleon' is less flavourful and classed as ornamental, while the green variety is the traditional culinary herb. Thanks to its strong flavour it tends not to be found in Canadian dishes unless they are very authentic. Add it to, you guessed it, fish dishes.

### ⑥ Red shiso
*Perilla frutescens*

Available in red or green, shiso is a quintessential Japanese edible that is used across Eastern Asia. It belongs to the mint family and thrives in the same conditions as basil. Shiso leaves are very expensive to buy, so if you want that authentic flavour without breaking the bank, growing it yourself is well worth it. The ruffled leaves of green shiso are used to serve wasabi, as a minced garnish, or in noodle dishes.

### ⑪ Lemon grass
*Cymbopogon citratus*

Popular in Asian cooking for centuries, this native of India has become popular in the West for its ease of growth and citrus tang. It can grow quite large (up to 1.8 m tall), but for container use simply cut it back once it reaches the height you want. It's tropical, so bring it indoors for winter. Use it to flavour almost any dish, especially those with Asian flair. The tea is said to ease coughs and upset stomach.

### ⑨ Banana 'Dwarf Cavendish'
*Musa acuminata*

'Cavendish' is one of the most ubiquitous supermarket bananas in the world. There are several dwarf types, ranging from a maximum height of 90 cm to 1.8 m. While the fruit is edible, it will take a few years to yield and is a bit seedy. Its leaves make an ideal and traditional wrap to cook Asian dishes, especially fish. When it does yield, the main rhizome will die and the suckers will have to take over, so don't cut them off.

### ⑩ Watercress
*Nasturtium officinale*

see p. 47

# DRAGON POTS
## Ingredients for Chinese Cuisine

**Height:** to 1 m

**CHINA IS ONE OF THE LARGEST** and most culturally diverse countries in the world. Its culinary traditions are so diverse and complex that it's impossible to call any one of them definitively Chinese.

In Canada, the Chinese food that is a staple of every shopping mall has become its own culinary style. Although it's loosely inspired by

Cantonese traditions, the majority of Chinese people wouldn't recognize the food that we've gotten used to. Just as the early Cantonese immigrants, who invented the style, worked with the vegetables that were available to them, I've chosen edibles for my container that you won't need to order from across the Pacific.

**A** Goji berry

**B** Anise-hyssop

**C** Lemon grass

**D** Bronze fennel

**E** Shallot

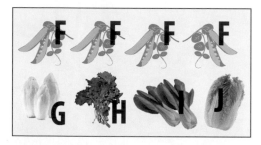

**F** Peas 'Little Sweetie'

**G** Endive

**H** Rapini

**I** Bok choi 'Toy Choi'

**J** Chinese cabbage

**Recommended container size:** 60 cm by 20 cm (2×)

This Asian herb container from Plant World in Toronto has lemon grass, Thai basil, cilantro and lemon balm.

This combination will want cooler temperatures than some of the hotter culinary combos, but it will still crave sunlight.

Goji berries are in the tomato family and are typically dried and cooked before being served with various dishes, including tea. There have been many claims about the health benefits of goji berries, but I was only able to find a handful of peer-reviewed studies to corroborate them.

I substituted rapini for the harder to find, but more authentic, Chinese broccoli (gai lan). Rapini is closely related and is an acceptable substitution in a stir-fry; it will taste more authentic than western broccoli.

Snow peas are used in countless Chinese dishes and are much tastier home-grown than store-bought. They aren't heavy plants and don't need much for a trellis. I used curly willow tips for a cheap support that is more decorative than mesh.

Under the peas, and shaded from the sun by their trellis, are the fresh greens that are integral to most Chinese dishes.

You can use the rapini and Chinese cabbage in your stir-fries. A word of caution concerning the Chinese cabbage: it likes to grow fast and broad, which makes more aggressive than the less aggressive bok choi

next to it. As it grew, I occasionally had to remove a lower cabbage leaf or three as they hogged the sunlight.

You'll find this effect with other edible plants, as well, including perennial strawberries, nasturtiums and even parsley. Never be afraid to remove an umbrella leaf that's threatening the health of the container.

Many Chinese edibles love the cool weather, so the two window boxes in this recipe peaked at different times. The peas and bok choi were a delicious June treat but petered just as the goji berry and fennel were beginning to shine.

Peas don't need an expensive trellis; they will climb string as long as you have some horizontal parts for them to gain leverage.

Curly willow makes an easy, affordable, attractive trellis. Snip off the weakest branches to prevent breakage.

You can buy seeds of mixed Asian greens that are ready to plant, like 'Stirfry Mix' from Renee's Garden.

## Cooking with these Pots

Most of these edibles are vegetables because, in many Chinese dishes, the vegetables best express the Asian flavours. If you want to explore growing

You can grow your own rice in beach pails on your patio, like the Artisan Sake Maker does on Granville Island in Vancouver.

more varieties, like Chinese eggplant and Chinese broccoli, you will need to look for seeds on the internet.

Most of the leafy vegetables here, like the bok choi, Chinese cabbage and endive, are exceptional in stir-fries. For traditional sauces, mushrooms and meats, don't be afraid to head to Chinatown, where the vendors have a fascinating array of edibles on offer. Make it part of the experience of cooking from your containers; going to the market to pick up fresh ingredients is an integral part of the Asian culinary culture.

## Chinese Greens

Chinese greens are exploding in popularity in Canada. Easy in the garden and versatile in the kitchen, they are helping a whole new generation discover that, when it comes to Chinese food, there is a world beyond ginger beef. My favourite way to have them is steamed or lightly stir-fried with some oyster sauce drizzled over top.

There are many types of greens available, and the nomenclature can get confusing. "Chinese cabbage" can seem to refer to one plant and a group of plants all at once. Don't let that discourage you.

Avoid the fruitless frustration of looking for starter plants. The seeds are readily available from large garden centres or online, and they germinate easily. With seeds, you also control your own destiny as far as sowing second crops goes.

Make sure the soil stays moist and cool; otherwise they will bolt into flower. I suggest using a natural mulch to cool the roots.

Whether it's mizuna, bok choi (also called pak choi), mustard greens or Chinese spinach, they all thrive in the same cool temperatures. These are spring and fall vegetables. They take less than two months from seed to plate. Plan for a spring crop that you sow either indoors (in cold regions) or outside as soon as the frosts lift. About two months from the first frosts in fall (again, depending on region), sow a fresh crop. Trying to grow them in summer will prove frustrating. You'll be watering all the time, worried when they flop over and play dead, and disappointed when the leaves are bitter.

Pak choi 'Green Fortune' from Renee's Garden is just one of the Asian greens that are easy to grow in cool spring weather.

### A Goji berry

*Lycium barbarum;* wolfberry

Goji is remarkably easy to grow once established. It can tolerate poor soils as long as it's not waterlogged; its aggressive root system allows it to tolerate drought, but it hates wet feet. Cold hardy, goji berry is hardy to most Canadian regions. It will grow to 2.4 m tall or more if you don't cut it back. Traditionally the berries are dried and cooked before being added to soups, meats or tea.

### B Anise-hyssop

*Agastache foeniculum*

see p. 46

### C Lemon grass

*Cymbopogon citratus*

see p. 71

### D Bronze fennel

*Foeniculum vulgare* 'Purpureum'

Used in a massive variety of dishes around the world, fennel is easy to grow and attracts swallowtail butterflies to your yard. Use the ferny bronze foliage in egg and vegetable dishes, or even to accent cut flower arrangements. The seeds have a licorice-like, anise flavour and make an excellent seasoning for fish. The flower head resembles dill and, culinary uses aside, the whole plant makes a delicate but eye-catching focal point in containers.

### E Shallot

*Allium oschaninii*

Native to Asia and closely related to multiplier onions, shallots are easy to grow and take up very little space in containers. You can buy offsets in packages or keep them from last year's crop. Plant so the pointy end is just breaking the surface; you don't want it fully submerged. Harvest when the tops begin to die back and/or flop over. Use as a subtler substitute for garlic or brown onions.

### Ⓕ Peas 'Little Sweetie'

*Pisum sativum;* snow peas

Snow peas have been cultivated in Southeast Asia for 12,000 years and are inescapable in numberless Asian dishes. They are one of the first vegetables you'll be grazing on in late spring; eat the peas, shell and all, before they ripen. Heat will slow down production, but it will bounce back in fall. Make sure to provide a trellis or choose a bushing variety; I usually opt for the trellis to save space.

### Ⓖ Endive

*Cichorium endivia*

Closely related to radicchio and chicory, endive comes in curled leaf and broad leaf types. It is rich in folate and vitamins. It's easy to grow (treat it like lettuce) and is excellent, though a bit bitter, in salads. It's more heat tolerant than lettuce but will still try to bolt in the heat. Harvest the complete head after about 80 days by chopping it at soil level, or harvest the leaves throughout the season.

### Ⓗ Rapini

*Brassica rapa ruvo;* broccolini

Rapini has long been a Mediterranean staple and is surging in Canadian popularity thanks to its peppery taste in salads and stir-fries. Make sure the soil doesn't dry out and watch for the buds to form on long stalks. Unlike supermarket broccoli, it forms many small heads instead of one large one. If it's hot outside the flowers will want to open quickly, wrecking the taste, so keep your eye on it.

### Ⓘ Bok choi 'Toy Choi'

*Brassica rapa* subsp. *chinensis*

This cultivar of bok choi tops out at only 13 cm tall, making it ideal for container growing. Bok choi is arguably the most popular Chinese green and is an indispensable part of an Asian edible garden. It loves cool temperatures, and you can start harvesting the leaves at any time. Stir-frying bok choi with garlic and soy sauce is an easy way to discover this classic Chinese vegetable.

### Ⓙ Chinese cabbage

*Brassica rapa* subsp. *pekinensis*

see p. 55

# BABYLONIAN FEAST
## Ingredients for Persian/Iranian Cuisine

**Height:** to 2 m

**NO EDIBLE CONTAINER GARDENING** book would be complete without a tribute to the original rooftop paradise, the fabled Hanging Gardens of Babylon. Built by Nebuchadnezzar II about 2700 years ago, this ancient wonder would have been a potent symbol of power and resources to friend and foe alike.

In this pot-bound microcosm I tried to capture a taste of the delicious beauty that the ancient gardens would have had. As I nibble on sweet figs, pomegranates and limes and smell Persian roses, I imagine what it would have been like for the king's wife, Amytis, as she wandered the opulence built by so many slaves.

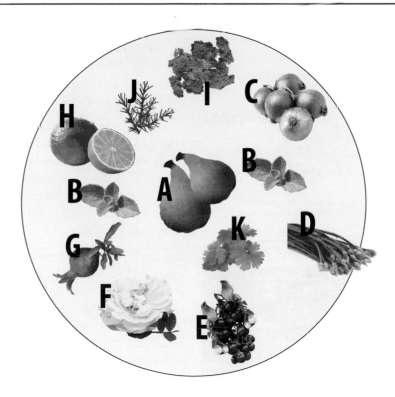

**A** Fig 'Italian Honey'

**B** Syrian oregano

**C** Onion 'Sweet Spanish'

**D** Garlic chives

**E** Tomato 'Tumbler'

**F** Rose 'Persian Yellow'

**G** Pomegranate 'Nana'

**H** Lime 'Persian'

**I** Parsley 'Triple Curled'

**J** Rosemary 'Tuscan Blue'

**K** Coriander/cilantro

**Recommended container size:**
70 cm across

Although inspired by the Babylonian Gardens, which sat in present day Iraq, the cuisine I tried to capture here also incorporates edibles from Iranian, or Persian, cooking. Both of these traditions originated in the fertile Mesopotamian valleys. Rumoured to be the home of the original Garden of Eden, this region contains much more than open desert. As an edible gardener, you have a tremendous diversity of plants to explore if you choose to focus on this culinary region.

The staples of Iraqi and Iranian cuisine tend to be cereals such as rice and meats such as lamb, none of which grow well in a container. Fruits such as figs, pomegranates and limes may take some homework to find, but once you have them they will last for years as winter houseplants and summer patio conversation starters.

In trying to mimic the layers of the Hanging Gardens, I chose a standard fig (no foliage on the bottom). When planning a container like this, remember that scale becomes important, and a rule of thumb is that the tallest plant should be twice as tall as the pot. Standard plants also save space at soil level.

I huddled a big Persian lime under the fig leaves. Its fruit, larger than key limes, are the classic green limes found in supermarkets. You could substitute a lemon, as it's used in many dishes as well.

The 'Nana' pomegranate is a dwarf variety and the fruit, though edible, is rather seedy. You should be able to find regular pomegranate bushes in large cities, but they will need more space. They will yield eventually, and you can move them in for winter and back out in spring like a fig.

Persian roses add colour, and with a little effort (and probably a few more roses), you can make your own rose water. Use it to flavour sweets like nougat and baklava; it is well worth the time involved.

The herbs range from common onions to exotic Syrian oregano, which is used in hummus, soups and dips. For those who love the crisp

The only downside to this planter is the lack of flowers. You may want to add nasturtiums to colour it up.

taste of tabbouleh, fresh parsley is a must. The tomatoes are meant to "tumble" down the side. Trailing plants are a rarity in the edibles world, so sometimes we need to be creative.

If you're feeling adventurous, there are many other ingredients that you could plant. Try making your next hummus from fresh-picked chickpeas, or your baba ghanoush with a patio-ripened eggplant.

Cilantro makes a spectacular centrepiece plant, but be aware that in the full, hot sun it will bolt quickly and die after it goes to seed.

Dwarf pomegranates are so seedy they are better for starting conversations than for eating. If you have the space, consider a larger variety.

## Cooking with these Pots

Both a single spice—Syrian oregano—and a collection of spices that includes sesame seed and sumac, za'atar is essential in Western and Central Asian cooking. Every region

Persian limes get about 6 cm wide and are solid green until they turn yellow when they ripen.

has its own version of the spice(s), so it can be hard to nail down exactly what za'atar is. It's used in hummus, soups and flatbread dips. It's most commonly dried and blended with thyme, savory and oregano.

As usual, herbs such as rosemary and Syrian oregano will be ready almost immediately. The larger fruits will take longer, depending on how many years old they are when you get them.

## Growing Figs

I'm willing to bet that it's been a while since you ate a fig right off the branch. That's a shame, because in Canada figs are one of the easiest and most rewarding exotic fruits to grow.

I've often wondered why fig trees aren't more popular as ornamental plants, even without the fruit. With their broad leaves, compact form and ease of growth, it's a wonder that they aren't fixtures in more sunrooms and backyards.

They thrive in containers. Call large garden centres around you and, if they don't carry figs, ask them to. The varieties sold by Canadian nurseries will be the compact, pot-loving types you're after.

Give them as much sun as possible and make sure they aren't too wet or dry. Fig leaves wilt easily, so try not to let them get there because it may impact the taste of the fruit. The figs themselves grow in the crooks where the branches meet the main stem.

A ripe fig will droop on the stem and turn from green to yellow or brown, depending on the variety. Be patient; they get sweeter as they ripen.

If you bring your fig tree in every winter, it will get large and very fruitful in a few seasons. Put the container on wheels if it gets too heavy.

It can be excruciating, but wait until the fruit is soft before picking it. I could suggest how to use it in the kitchen but, let's be honest, you're going to eat them before they even make it inside. And yes, they will be as delicious as you're imagining.

---

### Ⓐ Fig 'Italian Honey'
*Ficus carica*

Besides having the distinction of providing the first piece of clothing in the Old Testament, figs have a history that reaches back almost as far as humanity itself. 'Italian Honey' figs are ideal for Canada. They tolerate our cool spring nights and don't need pollination, meaning they can yield indoors. The fruit is irresistibly sweet and, if you keep them out of your mouth long enough, is ideal for jams or drying. Keep your tree year after year.

### Ⓑ Syrian oregano
*Origanum vulgare* var. *syriacum;* Bible hyssop

This ancient herb appears in Psalm 51:7. Unlike the creeping Greek oregano, the Syrian variety grows to a stately height of 90 cm when it bursts into bloom. Pinch off the flavourful young leaves to keep it compact in your container and to enjoy in a multitude of dishes. The pungent taste is similar to Greek oregano, but the leaves have a rugged, silver tinge that makes it more ornamental than the Greek.

### Ⓒ Onion 'Sweet Spanish'
*Allium cepa;* Spanish onion

Humans have eaten onions since at least 5000 BCE. They are easy to grow in a container at least 30 cm deep. Spanish onions have a sweeter, mellower flavour than their hotter, harsher cousins. Some people (I'm not one of them) like eating the baseball-sized bulbs like apples because they have so much flavour. Consider Spanish onions when you don't want an overpowering onion taste.

### Ⓓ Garlic chives
*Allium tuberosum*

see p. 55

### Ⓔ Tomato 'Tumbler'
*Lycopersicon lycopersicum*

see p. 229

###  Rose 'Persian Yellow'
*Rosa foetida*

As there are no native yellow roses in Europe, gardeners were excited when this yellow one was brought from Persia. It boasts pretty yellow flowers that appear once a year in early summer. The smell isn't what you expect from a rose and takes some getting used to. This isn't the best variety for container growing; I included it for authenticity. For a showier rose, choose a more compact, freer blooming variety.

###  Pomegranate 'Nana'
*Punica granatum*

Native to modern-day Iraq and Iran, the pomegranate has always been intertwined with human civilization. This dwarf variety bears small fruits that are often too seedy to eat, but it's perfect for growing in containers. You can grow the regular cultivar as long as you have a lot of space to give it. Make sure to bring it in for winter. It's very drought tolerant and gets very few pests.

###  Lime 'Persian'
*Citrus latifolia;* Persian lime, Tahiti lime

Persian limes are larger than Key limes and have a less intense citrus flavour. They are thornless and usually seedless, with the large fruit having a long shelf life (which makes it the preferred lime for commercial growing). It's as much a houseplant as a patio plant and will grow, though probably not yield, indoors over winter as long as it has a sunny spot.

### Parsley 'Triple Curled'
*Petroselinum crispum*

see p. 171

### Rosemary 'Tuscan Blue'
*Rosmarinus officinalis*

see p. 217

### Coriander/cilantro
*Coriandrum sativum*

While North Americans call the leaves of this plant "cilantro" and the seeds "coriander," to the rest of the world the whole plant is simply coriander. It boasts broad, white flowers and has lot of presence in containers. If given enough space it will reach 1.5 m tall or more. The dried seeds are a spice with a nutty, citrusy flavour popular in Asian cooking and pickling, while the leaves are an acquired taste.

# THAT'S AMORE
## Ingredients for Italian Cuisine

**Height:** to 1.5 m

**WE LIVE HECTIC LIVES.** Catching five minutes between office deadlines, soccer practice and mowing the lawn to scarf down some food can reduce eating to more of a chore than a pleasure.

In Italy, food and culture are interwoven in so many areas that it's impossible to separate one from the other. The Italians invented the "Slow Food" movement, and we could learn a lot from them about how to slow down and relish an afternoon devoted to fresh flavours, good company and delicious food.

- **A**   Tomato 'Roma'
- **B**   Italian parsley
- **C**   Basil
- **D**   Florence fennel
- **E**   Radicchio
- **F**   Coriander/cilantro
- **G**   Rosemary 'Tuscan Blue'
- **H**   Tomato 'Tumbler'
- **I**   Rapini
- **J**   Olive 'Arbequina'
- **K**   English thyme
- **L**   Sage
- **M**   Artichoke 'Imperial Star'
- **N**   Mint 'Italian Spice'

**Recommended container size:** 50 cm across / 40 cm across / 35 cm across

---

Draw a diagram of your containers when you plant them so that you have a record of what you did for the next year.

This ended up being a massive combination because I couldn't decide which edibles I could do without. Each time I thought of not including one I remembered a favourite dish that depended on it. As it is, I'm missing lemons and pomegranates, which are pivotal to the southern Italian diet.

Italian food is highly regional. The country has a multitude of distinct cultural and climatic zones, and many areas have culinary traditions that are thousands of years old.

These are all heat lovers and, although the olive might take some calls, easy to find in large garden centres. You'll easily find seed for radicchio and rapini, along with a host of other varieties that I haven't included.

You may need to keep an eye on the coriander and artichoke because they will need to get large before they mature. I nestled the artichoke under a standard-trained olive, hoping that they could co-exist in such a small pot.

Very few specific varieties are as tied to a country as the 'Roma' tomato is to Italy. It's the essential tomato for pasta sauce, so don't accept substitutions. It's a determinate type, meaning it will grow to a certain size and stop, making it ideal for containers.

Try to plant at least one basil plant wherever you have a tomato. In one of the most classic companion planting love stories, basil helps tomatoes repel insects and improves their growth and flavour. Basil also pairs well with peppers, oregano and asparagus. Don't plant basil with rue or sage.

Fennel has a reputation for being the bad kid that doesn't play well with other edibles in mixed containers. I added it hesitatingly to mixed pots and watched it closely, but found no evidence that it was inhibiting the other plants' growth, despite its reputation. As a bonus, planting "fennel near your kennel" will help to keep fleas from your pooches.

Don't expect your artichoke to produce lots of fruit. Enjoy the massive plant and think of the fruit as a bonus.

Create an Italian herb garden with basil, fennel, rosemary, parsley, oregano, thyme, sage, bay and marjoram like this one from Plant World in Toronto.

'Roma' is the most popular plum tomato, but there are many more, like 'Italian Pompeii' from Renee's Garden.

## Cooking with these Pots

Most classic Italian dishes don't have a lot of ingredients and aren't complicated to make. Their success hinges on the quality and freshness of the individual ingredients. In growing your own edibles, you're already one giant step toward embracing the spirit of Italian cooking. As you prepare and enjoy the food, stay within that tradition by taking time to appreciate the increased taste that home-grown edibles bring.

If there are certain recipes that you want to grow, make and eat again and again, feel free to customize the mix. Add a bell pepper to make pizza or an extra 'Roma' tomato for a big batch of pasta sauce.

## Growing Olives

With their lance-like, silver tinged foliage and undemanding growth, it's surprising that Canadian gardeners haven't taken to olive trees in a bigger way. As intimidating as the name sounds, conjuring images of ancient groves adorning hills in the Holy Land, they are actually quite easy to grow in containers.

To get started, call around to large garden centres to find out who has them. Like figs, the varieties that Canadian nurseries are growing will tend to be compact, early-fruiting types hybridized specifically for container growing. If you have a choice, I suggest 'Arbequina' for beginners because it's easy to prune and bears prolific fruit very early.

Olive flowers are daintily beautiful and rain pollen if you tap them. They appear *en masse* in spring.

Olives aren't high maintenance. Give your olive plenty of hot sun and let it dry slightly between waterings. Apply nitrogen-rich fertilizer a few times a year; slow-release types will give the best response for your money.

The only tricky part about getting an olive to fruit is that it isn't a full-out tropical plant and needs to be chilled over winter. In fall, leave it outside long enough to expose it to cool days and light frosts but bring it indoors as soon as the temperature drops below -5° C. If you're not an olive fan and aren't interested in getting fruit, this step becomes optional.

Pruning olives is fairly simple. The goal is for the branches to be shaped upward like a vase. You want an open, airy feel, so clear out unproductive growth or branches too close to each other. Lastly, eliminate any suckers that grow at the base.

The fruit starts as creamy white flowers that send a plume of delicate pollen into the air when touched. They don't need a pollinator, though bees will help to increase the yield. Depending on your taste you can pick the olives when green or let them ripen to black.

---

### Ⓐ **Tomato 'Roma'**
*Lycopersicon lycopersicum*

These plum tomatoes are indispensable in pasta and pizza sauce. They have a distinct pear shape and are often found in supermarkets (though those ones won't be as tasty as yours). Being determinate tomatoes, they won't grow to massive sizes and will need minimal support. They have very few seeds and are excellent for canning. Harvest when the fruit is uniformly red from base to tip.

### ⓑ Italian parsley

*Petroselinum crispum* var. *neapolitanum;* flat-leaf parsley

'Triple Curled' parsley looks prettier in containers, but it's the stronger-flavoured Italian variety that has become the darling of the cooking set. It can look spindly and a bit awkward in a container, especially next to its manicured garnish cousin, but it makes up for that in the kitchen. Add fresh leaves to homemade pesto, marinara, bruschetta or lasagne. It's also more forgiving of adverse growing conditions than 'Triple Curled' parsley.

### ⓒ Basil

*Ocimum basilicum*

see p. 127

### ⓓ Florence fennel

*Foeniculum vulgare* var. *azoricum;* finocchio

The anise-flavoured, fleshy bulb that Florence fennel produces is a home-grown rarity in Canada because it's darn tricky. Make sure you get the vegetable fennel seed (not the herb, which is easier to grow), and it needs to be direct seeded because it hates being transplanted. I only recommend growing it in warmer regions because, if faced with cool nights or serious temperature fluctuations, it will bolt to flower and *poof* goes the flavour. That being said, the bulb is delicious in salads.

### ⓔ Radicchio

*Cichorium intybus;* Italian chicory

Radicchio is a beautiful salad green that will bring rich red, splotchy leaves to a container. Use it sparingly when fresh, as it has a strong spicy taste to it. The bitterness mellows when you cook it. It's very nutritious and is high in potassium. Like most leafy greens, try to grow it in a cool spot. If it's in a container, shade it with a cucumber, tomato or other beefy sun lover.

### ⓕ Coriander/cilantro

*Coriandrum sativum*

see p. 87

### ⓖ Rosemary 'Tuscan Blue'

*Rosmarinus officinalis*

see p. 217

### ⓗ Tomato 'Tumbler'
*Lycopersicon lycopersicum*

see p. 229

### ⓘ Rapini
*Brassica rapa ruvo*

see p. 79

### ⓙ Olive 'Arbequina'
*Olea europaea;* Spanish olive

Olives have been known to bear fruit for 500 years from a single tree. Although they normally take five to 10 years to bear fruit, 'Arbequina' is a compact variety that fruits in about three years. It has a weeping habit and makes a great ornamental tree for sunny patios. Bring it indoors over winter and prune as needed. It is wind pollinated so you don't need two trees, though having more than one will increase yield.

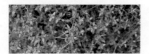

### ⓚ English thyme
*Thymus vulgaris*

see p. 209

### ⓛ Sage
*Salvia officinalis*

see p. 62

### ⓜ Artichoke 'Imperial Star'
*Cynara scolymus*

Closely related to the common thistle, artichokes are architecturally stirring plants that create edible buds that look like armoured spheres. 'Imperial Star' yields in the first season. Give it plenty of space, fertilizer and time to mature; plant seeds indoors months before the last frost. You can bring it indoors over winter. It probably won't yield much the first year, but it will get bigger after that.

### ⓝ Mint 'Italian Spice'
*Mentha* hybrids

'Italian Spice' mint contains hints of marjoram and oregano and makes an excellent seasoning in pasta and pizza sauces. Like other mints, it prefers some afternoon shade and can take over if not regularly snipped. Mint tends to lose its taste when grown from seed, so buy starter plants. This one is available from Richters herbs.

# DINNER WITH ZORBA
## Ingredients for Greek Cuisine

**Height:** to 2 m

**THERE'S SOMETHING INNATELY** soothing about Greek food. Whether it's dipping into crisp tzatziki or enjoying a cool Greek salad, it has the ability to bring a little bit of the Greek beach to our plates.

The warm Greek climate has led to the cultivation of an abundant array of fruits and vegetables, resulting in dishes that are as colourful as the culture itself. These containers are celebrations of flavour, freshness and the indomitable Greek spirit.

Ⓐ Fig 'Texas Everbearing'

Ⓑ Greek oregano

Ⓒ Spearmint

Ⓓ Olive

Ⓔ Rosemary 'Tuscan Blue'

Ⓕ Cucumber 'Long English'

Ⓖ Arugula

Ⓗ Dill 'Bouquet'

Ⓘ Eggplant 'Amethyst'

Ⓙ Basil

Ⓚ Tomato 'Sungold'

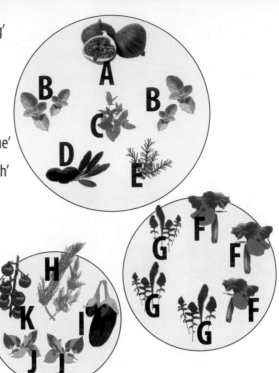

**Recommended container size:** 50 cm across / 40 cm across / 35 cm across

If you're planting containers in a theme, try matching the pots with the theme, like these terracotta resin pots for my Greek look.

The roots of Greek cooking run deep. Greece lies at the geographical confluence of Europe and the Middle East, making it the natural meeting place for disparate culinary influences. Traditions from Italy, Turkey, the Balkans and Syria have merged in Greece to create dishes that cherish fresh ingredients while never shying away from exotic flavours.

You'll be able to find most of these edibles in larger garden centres, though you may need to call around for the olive and fig. They are all high yielding, and these few containers will provide a lot of food throughout summer, whether you cook with it or end up grazing on the patio.

The edibles that like life on the dry side, including the figs and olives, are in their own container. Let the soil surface of that container dry slightly, but keep the other containers evenly moist (self-watering pots are ideal).

Just like the Greeks, these containers like it hot. Place them in the hottest spots you have on your patio or deck, preferably where the sun can ricochet off some siding. Make sure to position the cucumber trellis so that it shades the cool-weather-loving arugula.

You may find that the arugula bolts quickly and turns bitter in the mid-summer heat, even with the cucumber shading it. Like many greens, it performs best in cool temperatures. Since it matures in 40 days, I suggest a spring crop (as early as is feasible), followed by flowers or another heat lover over summer, followed by a fall crop in early September.

I made these containers for cooking, but the reality is that many of the ingredients are made for grazing. How can you resist plucking ripe figs off your patio and eating them on the spot? If you're a fan of one dish that you plan to prepare, plan in advance so that you don't nibble off all the cucumbers a week before making tzatziki.

This Mediterranean-themed planter from Plant World in Toronto features lavender, marjoram, oregano, rosemary, sage, bay, basil, savory and thyme.

There seems to be no end to the shapes, sizes and colours of tomato hybrids available, like these 'Mini Pears' from Renee's Garden.

The ingredients in these containers are hardy and substantial enough to fit in well alongside any Greek dish. There aren't a lot of herbs here, but between the cucumbers, tomatoes and figs, there's more than enough to fill you up.

## Cooking with these Pots

Many of these heat-loving edibles are heavy producers and are best used immediately after picking. The success of Greek recipes such as moussaka largely depend on the freshness of the ingredients (in that case, eggplant), so try to time your cooking with the fruit ripening. The 'Amethyst' eggplant is the larger type used in traditional moussaka.

You have almost everything you need for a fresh Greek salad here, lacking only green bell peppers and, of course, feta. Imagine serving a salad to your guests or family having picked almost all of it off your patio.

I included the 'Long English' cucumber partially because it has a sweet skin and doesn't need peeling. Some Greek dishes call specially for unpeeled cucumbers. For homemade donairs, you may want to substitute a 'Roma' or 'Early Girl' tomato for the 'Sungold' cherry tomato.

Pickling is enjoying a resurgence in popularity as a new generation is discovering that it's easier than they thought it was.

## Making Olive Oil

Once your olive tree starts to bear significant amounts of fruit, adventurous gardeners can dive into thousands of years of tradition and make their own olive oil. It's time consuming but not overly difficult, and imagine what your guests will say when you tell them they're dipping their bread in homemade olive oil.

Make sure you start with a decent amount of olives, as each olive will yield only about 4 grams of oil. If you need to supplement with store-bought olives, go to a Greek or Italian market and look for the freshest olives that best match your own.

Wait until your olive tree is brimming with fruit and pick them right before you press them. This is important because olives start losing their flavour the moment they are picked. It's also why your homemade oil will be so delicious.

There are quite a few steps, but the short form is that you need to mash, pulp and squish the olives to extract the oil. There are many ways to do this, and depending on how traditional you want to be you can use anything from

Olives start out looking like tiny clusters of grapes on the stem, and slowly mature in the summer sun.

cheesecloth and stones to a blender and colander.

However you do it, waiting for the oil to emerge is a lesson in patience.

Once it's finished and you take your first taste, the reason why Mediterranean peoples have been doing it for thousands of years will suddenly be clear.

### Ⓐ Fig 'Texas Everbearing'
*Ficus carica;* Turkish fig

This fig is ideal for warmer Canadian regions; if warm enough, it will yield throughout summer and into fall. The fruit is reddish brown and slightly sweet. Bring it indoors before the first frost and give it as much direct light as possible throughout the year. It needs to be fertilized every month or two in the growing season, but don't give it too much nitrogen or you'll only get leaves and no fruit. It yields at a young age and stays compact in containers. Established trees in large pots produce surprisingly large crops.

### Ⓑ Greek oregano
*Origanum vulgare* var. *hirtum;* wild marjoram

For its culinary versatility and ease of growth, oregano is one of our most beloved herbs. It's almost impossible to imagine Mediterranean or Middle Eastern cuisine without oregano. 'Greek' is an attractive dark green, low-growing plant with softly textured leaves. Its earthy, aromatic taste will get stronger if you dry the leaves, and it is delicious with almost anything. Oregano also acts as an antiseptic and has ample antioxidants.

### Ⓒ Spearmint
*Mentha spicata;* English mint

I've never met anyone who couldn't grow spearmint. Keep some moisture in the soil and this little plant does the rest. It's so easy that if you don't confine it to a container you won't be able to get rid of it. Add a leaf to your iced tea, make fresh mint sauce for your lamb, or add to any number of other dishes—it has many uses.

### Ⓓ Olive
*Olea europaea*

see p. 95

### Ⓔ Rosemary 'Tuscan Blue'
*Rosmarinus officinalis*

see p. 217

### F Cucumber 'Long English'
*Cucumis sativus*

see p. 111

### G Arugula
*Eruca vesicaria* subsp. *sativa;* rocket

Arugula has been used as an aphrodisiac for 2000 years. It boasts deeply lobed leaves and makes an attractive alternative to lettuce. It has a surprisingly strong, peppery taste that is used for flavouring as much as for a simple salad green. Add it to salads to liven up the lettuce, or lay some fresh leaves on your pizza for an extra layer of taste.

### H Dill 'Bouquet'
*Anethum graveolens*

I always make an excuse to brush past dill, just to smell the wonderful fragrance that gets stirred up. Although its fame comes from its pickling prowess, its aromatic leaves can flavour fish, soups and veggies. 'Bouquet' is more compact than the giant garden dill and is best for container use, topping out around 1 m tall. The yellow seed heads are symmetrically gorgeous; allow them to dry on the plants before collecting the seed.

### I Eggplant 'Amethyst'
*Solanum melongena;* aubergine

Eggplant is an Indian native and has been cultivated there for thousands of years. Although the fruit is bitter when fresh, cooking improves the flavour and it has a host of culinary uses. It can be stuffed, stewed, roasted, grilled and more. 'Amethyst' has been bred specifically for containers. With tactile leaves, papery, purple flowers and smooth, almost black-skinned fruit, it has a lot of beauty to bring to a container.

### J Basil
*Ocimum basilicum*

see p. 127

### K Tomato 'Sungold'
*Lycopersicon lycopersicum*

People who grow 'Sungold' once almost always grow it again and again. It's a vigorous indeterminate (needs staking) variety that produces scores of apricot orange cherry tomatoes that you'll be eating right off the vine. Make sure to let them ripen fully so that the fruit fills with sugars. Use them fresh to add colour and taste to almost anything from salads to pizzas.

# JOLLY GOOD
## Ingredients for British Cuisine

**Height:** to 2 m

**HAVE YOU EVER NOTICED** how many of the most popular celebrity chefs are British? It's more than the nifty accent. They exude an appreciation of flavour and quality of ingredients. The desire to always seek out a better-tasting carrot and cucumber is a big part of making, and appreciating, great food.

Although contemporary cuisine in Britain has assimilated the flavours and styles of the various cultures that have come to call it home, British cooking is known for being unfussy. Chefs across the United Kingdom use simple sauces and seasonings to accentuate the robust flavours of high-quality, home-grown ingredients.

**A** Crabapple 'Dreamweaver'

**B** Borage

**C** Chives

**D** Viola 'Penny Mix'

**E** Calendula 'Bon Bon Mix'

**F** Blackberry 'Prime-Ark 45'

**G** Cucumber 'Long English'

**H** Beets 'Red Ace'

**I** Carrots 'Rainbow Mix'

**J** Scarlet runner beans

**Recommended container size:** 60 cm by 60 cm (2×) / 50 cm across

When I told people I was making a combination of British ingredients, I encountered more than a little skepticism. Once they saw the final product, that skepticism vanished. This combination, with fresh fruit, root vegetables, beans and cucumbers, is a celebration of good, simple food. You won't find finicky recipes here.

Scarlet runner beans might just be the easiest edible to grow, and they are delicious cooked with a little (or a lot of) butter.

These 'Golden Gourmet' beets from Renee's Garden would look sensational in a warm fall salad.

Carrots may seem an odd match with cucumbers as the former thrives in cool temperatures and the latter loves heat waves. The combination only works well with some slick positioning that incorporates the direction of the sun. Make sure the cucumber plant, with its trellis, is facing south. The goal is that, once the hot weather arrives, the leaves will be large enough to shade the carrots (and beets) and cool them off.

Beets will add minerals to the soil that will benefit the plants growing around them. As both they and carrots are cool-season veggies, you may want to add a warmer crop once they've matured.

I positioned the sun-loving blackberry on the western side to siphon off the late afternoon scorch. If overwintering blackberry bushes isn't worth the fruit, consider raspberries instead (just don't plant them together). For something even easier, plant strawberries.

Besides being one of the tastiest vegetables, runner beans are also among the easiest to grow. They need a trellis, but this is an easy fix; they climb just about anything. They grow up to 6 m in a season and make an ideal privacy screen to shield from nosy neighbours.

Clusters of about a dozen eye-catching red flowers precede the beans, which grow into long green fingers hanging off the stems. The beans get tough if left on the stem too long, so make sure to pick them before they fully ripen. If they are too tough, shell them before eating. The beans contain traces of lectin, which you'll need to neutralize by cooking before eating.

There's so much more to carrots than orange. There's a rainbow of varieties available, like this 'Tricolor Mix' from Renee's Garden.

## Cooking with these Pots

British cooks know the value of simple, tasty ingredients. Whether it's a boiled beet or meringues with fresh blackberries, they let the flavour speak for itself, and it works brilliantly.

I encourage you to take the time to taste the flavour that home growth makes. Whether it's carrots to go beside the Yorkshire puddings on Sunday or blackberries and clotted cream for tea, growing your own food will connect you with the earthy, robust spirit of the culture.

From crabapples to sour cherries, making jam and jelly preserves is one of the sweetest ways to capture summer in a jar.

## Apples in Pots

Many urbanites who don't have a yard have given up on being able to eat apples fresh off the stem. They don't have to. With a little overwintering know-how, columnar apples are ideal for small, sunny patios and will give you fresh fruit year after year.

I chose a crabapple, but there are several varieties of larger apples that will thrive in containers. As you will be overwintering it in a pot, try to choose a variety that is at least one zone better than where you are (so if you're in zone 5, choose a variety approved for zone 4 or lower).

Make sure your apple tree is in as large a container as possible and water it well before it freezes. The roots need to be like popsicle sticks encased in ice. Balconies on high rises can be brutal for winterizing plants thanks to the high winds, so if you live on one make sure to provide lots of wind protection by wrapping the pot well with tarp or burlap.

Bees are essential for a good apple crop, so I planted borage and other flowers around the apple to attract them—and as a bonus, the flowers are edible. A good hearty buzzing sound means a good yield ahead.

Try to keep your apple tree away from any cedars. Cedar-apple rust is a nasty fungus that starts as a gooey orange blob on cedars and moves to apples, damaging yields and trees. Your tree will be safe if isolated from cedars.

Planting chives with apples will help deter the dreaded apple scab from ruining your crop. The beneficial

The Montreal Botanical Garden inspired me with their collection of orchards in makeshift containers using only burlap and supports.

effect is so significant that spraying apple trees with a strong chive tea will help protect it from scab. Chive tea will also ward powdery mildew off cucumber leaves.

---

### Ⓐ Crabapple 'Dreamweaver'
*Malus* spp.

Columnar apples are ideal container growers because they stay compact (usually 3–3.6 m tall at maturity) and yield a surprising amount of fruit. 'Dreamweaver' has gorgeous pink flowers, but the fruit is tart; choose a larger apple if you're looking for sweeter fruit. Its maximum width is 90 cm, so you won't need to prune much. Pick up any unused apples to prevent apple maggot.

### Ⓑ Borage
*Borago officinalis;* starflower

Borage tops my list of most under-appreciated herbs, and I want to bring it back into the mainstream. Easy to grow and gorgeous, it sends up scores of purple-blue flowers that the bees flock to. Its cucumber taste refreshes a salad, and it is also the traditional garnish for one of my favourite cocktails, the Pimms cup. If nothing else, it increases pollination levels of plants around it. Wear gloves when handling it if you have sensitive skin.

### Ⓒ Chives
*Allium schoenoprasum*

see p. 171

### Ⓓ Viola 'Penny Mix'
*Viola* hybrids

see p. 119

### Ⓔ Calendula 'Bon Bon Mix'
*Calendula officinalis;* pot marigold

Although it's commonly called pot marigold, calendula is more closely related to daises than marigolds. Its soft, touchable flowers bloom all summer, and its cheerful colour makes it an essential edible flower. It is easy to grow and branches out to bloom profusely even as you nip the flowers. Harvest flowers in early morning and use the petals fresh in salads or as a garnish. If you're going to eat them, start from seed and avoid it while pregnant.

### **F** Blackberry 'Prime-Ark 45'

*Rubus fruticosus*

Growing blackberries in containers is possible but requires some advance planning. They fruit on second-year canes, so you will need to overwinter them in pots. 'Prime-Ark 45' is a flavourful, thorny variety that is hardy to zone 4, which makes overwintering it in pots much eas ier (especially in zone 5). It has midnight black fruit and loves cool temperatures; heat waves can interfere with its yield. Prune out old growth.

### **G** Cucumber 'Long English'

*Cucumis sativus*

These are my favourite cukes because they are so easy to eat right out of the garden. Regularly over 30 cm long, their skin is sweeter than other varieties and their near lack of seeds makes them very easy to digest. A sturdy trellis is a must. Get them as hot as possible and try to keep water off the leaves to avoid fungal disease. Don't let the soil dry out.

### **H** Beets 'Red Ace'

*Beta vulgaris*

see p. 147

### **I** Carrots 'Rainbow Mix'

*Daucus carota*

A thousand years ago we grew a host of multi-coloured carrots. It wasn't until we started to selectively breed them that we were fooled into thinking orange is the only colour. Carrots are easy in a container as long as it's at least 30 cm deep and has well-draining soil. Just like in the garden, thin out the delicious baby carrots so the others can grow big. I usually sprinkle fresh seeds as I go.

### **J** Scarlet runner beans

*Phaseolus coccineus*

Fresh runner beans are one of the true treats of summer. Pretty enough to be grown as an ornamental plant, they thrive in the warm soil of containers and grow very quickly. Forget about transplants; direct seed at the base of a trellis (any trellis). I just stuck some curly willow into the soil and watched them climb. Harvesting frequently will keep them blooming. The beans contain traces of toxic lectin, so make sure to cook them before eating.

# SALSA TIME

**Height:** to 1 m • **Spread:** to 60 cm

**IF YOU WANT TO SHOW** off your edible gardening prowess but don't consider yourself to be a pro, try growing ingredients for making your own salsa. The plants are easy to grow, and it's one of the rare dishes that you can grow everything that goes into it on your patio.

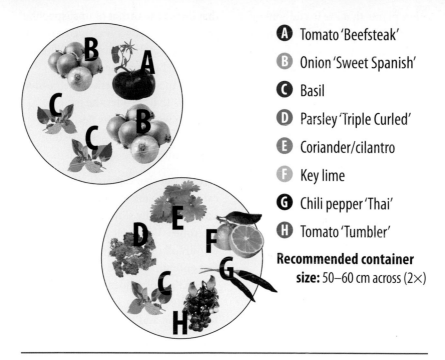

**A** Tomato 'Beefsteak'

**B** Onion 'Sweet Spanish'

**C** Basil

**D** Parsley 'Triple Curled'

**E** Coriander/cilantro

**F** Key lime

**G** Chili pepper 'Thai'

**H** Tomato 'Tumbler'

**Recommended container size:** 50–60 cm across (2×)

The word *salsa* is simply Spanish for "sauce," and there are countless variations across cultures based on local ingredients and tastes. I've chosen ingredients for *pico de gallo*, a classic Mexican salsa that literally translates as "rooster's beak." Its flavours come from fresh, raw ingredients, and it is typically spicy with a twist of lime.

A great thing about salsa is its versatility. It's so simple that you can easily adapt the ingredients to your taste. If you don't want as much spice, replace the chilis with sweet 'Mariachi' peppers. Conversely, if you're a glutton for punishment, use dwarf and deadly habaneros.

The 'Beefsteak' tomato is a statement maker but will require a large support structure and a lot of water when it gets larger. I heartily recommend a self-watering container with as large a reservoir as possible. Make sure to provide support that's both strong and adjustable as the plant grows vertically.

If you're planting in a peat moss–based medium, sprinkle dried, crushed eggshells into the soil to provide calcium. Doing so helps with blossom end rot, which loves to strike 'Beefsteaks.' If 'Beefsteaks' sound like too much work for salsa, try 'Early Girl' or, for a yellow twist, 'Lemon Boy' tomatoes instead.

If you don't like the smell of cilantro leaves, you're not alone. Aphids hate it too and they will usually avoid any other plants that are in the container with it. Coriander inhibits seed formation in fennel, so keep the two plants away from each other.

I planted some 'Triple Curled' parsley largely because it grows beneficially with tomatoes. Chop it fine and it will add texture and a fresh, tangy taste to your salsa.

## Why Chilies Are Hot

Evolutionarily speaking, peppers shouldn't be spicy. Plants typically grow fruit in order to offer a meal to animals, who then help scatter the seeds. So why would a plant want to grow bright, delicious-looking fruit

Thai peppers are easy to grow and aren't excessively hot, which makes them versatile in the kitchen.

that burns the throat of unsuspecting critters? The answer was uncovered by researchers at the University of Florida in 2008. The arch enemy of wild peppers in South America is *Fusarium*, a fungus that invades the fruit through wounds on its flesh. Once inside it destroys the seeds before larger animals can spread them.

It turns out that capsaicin, the chemical we can thank for making peppers painful, rapidly slows the growth of microbes. When *Fusarium* attacks a chili full of capsaicin, it can't grow fast enough to destroy the seeds. While the spice does deter mammals from the peppers, birds are immune to the heat and can eat their fill.

Capsaicin's ability to slow microbial growth has massive implications to human health. Almost every culture near the equator has used hot peppers for centuries to flavour and preserve their food. As anyone who has taken a bite out of the wrong pepper knows, they really clear your sinuses. Eating spicy peppers regularly is a great way to ease congestion and protect yourself from bronchitis.

---

### 🅐 Tomato 'Beefsteak'
*Lycopersicon lycopersicum*

The largest commonly available tomato, 'Beefsteak' fruit regularly tops 0.5 kg. It's a large indeterminate, so make sure to give it lots of space and support. The kidney-shaped fruit takes a long time to develop, but if need be you can bring the green tomatoes indoors to ripen. They're perfect sliced for sandwiches and diced for salsa. Fertilize regularly and keep the soil slightly moist to prevent the fruit from splitting.

### ⓑ Onion 'Sweet Spanish'
*Allium cepa*

see p. 86

### ⓒ Basil
*Ocimum basilicum*

see p. 127

### ⓓ Parsley 'Triple Curled'
*Petroselinum crispum*

see p. 171

### ⓔ Coriander/cilantro
*Coriandrum sativum*

see p. 87

### ⓕ Key lime
*Citrus aurantifolia*

Compared to the ubiquitous Persian lime, Key limes are smaller, more tart and yellow when ripe. They provide tangy flavour to fish, marinades and alcoholic drinks. Canadians love them because they perform well in northern climates, being small enough (90 cm to 1.5 m tall) to move inside in winter. Key limes aren't easy to find in supermarkets, so if you're a key lime pie purist, growing them is the way to go.

### ⓖ Chili pepper 'Thai'
*Capsicum annuum*

Although chilis may seem exotic to us, they are a daily menu item for the majority of the world's population. 'Thai' chili peppers are little heat lovers with a big kick. You can keep them year after year as long as they have ample sun indoors over winter, and they don't grow very large. The curved, pendulous peppers (usually red) can approach habanero heat at up to 100,000 Scoville units.

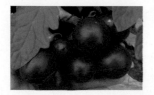

### ⓗ Tomato 'Tumbler'
*Lycopersicon lycopersicum*

see p. 229

# GARDEN OF EARTHLY DELIGHTS

**Height:** to 1.5 m • **Spread:** to 1 m    /

**WHAT COULD BE MORE** satisfying than having all the ingredients for a fresh salad in one container? Being able to pull tonight's salad right off your patio is what edible container gardening is all about. Keep this container close to the door so you can harvest a little and harvest often.

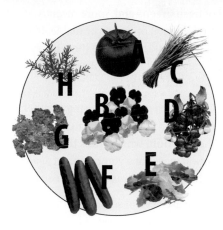

**A** Tomato 'Early Girl'

**B** Viola 'Penny Mix'

**C** Chives

**D** Tomato 'Tumbler'

**E** Lettuce 'Asian Baby Leaf'

**F** Cucumber 'Pot Luck'

**G** Parsley 'Triple Curled'

**H** Rosemary 'Tuscan Blue'

**Recommended container size:** 60–70 cm across

We often plant containers of annuals according to playful themes, like a tropical theme, a mix of purples or a scented garden. Themes work with edible containers as well, but they tend to reflect taste palates instead of colour palettes.

This recipe overflows with a salad blend of lettuce and mesclun, abundant 'Early Girl' tomatoes, miniature 'Pot Luck' cucumbers, chives and even violas for colourful garnish. It's designed to yield small amounts (enough for a few salads) again and again throughout summer.

From a design perspective, it's a robust combination that makes a statement on the patio. While the violas add a blue twist, the real beauty comes from the luscious greens that splash against each other. The soft chartreuse lettuce accents the deep green tomato plant. Throw in some broad cucumber leaves and crisp, vertical chives and it's a visually dynamic mix.

You'll want to give this recipe a lot of sunlight, but if possible try to position it so the tomato is on the southwest side. It will then provide some shade to the more sensitive salad greens and violas.

You can grow as much food on your patio as you can in a garden, and there will always be something harvest-ready and tasty nearby.

Salad greens are one of the easiest edibles to grow and yield enormous amounts for the small amount of energy they require.

Lettuce grows beneficially with cucumbers, strawberries and carrots. It also helps onions develop their bulbs.

## Harvesting Fresh Greens

Leafy greens are one of the easiest and cheapest crops to grow in containers. Even the exotic varieties, such as mesclun and mizuna, are affordable and go a long way. They infuse pots with an automatic lushness and often provide coloured or textured leaves to add variety.

Choosing what variety to plant used to be a choice between spinach, green lettuce or red lettuce. In the past decade there's been an explosion

of fresh greens and, more recently, fresh blends of greens available. If you're thinking outside the lettuce, Renee's Garden specializes in whimsical salad mixes.

Greens thrive in cool spring weather. In the summer heat it's natural for them to bolt, which ruins the flavour. In warm regions you can plant again at the end of August for fall salads.

There are several schools of thought when it comes to how to harvest greens in order to achieve the best balance of volume and flavour. The classic way is to harvest outside leaves a few at a time, working your way to the emerging centre. You'll get a lot of leaves this way but, because you're taking mature growth, not as much flavour.

Cut-and-come-again is a new method that gives the best of both worlds. You essentially treat the greens like lawn, cutting them off when they reach 10–15 cm tall but leaving 5 cm behind. Most varieties will regrow three or even four times, allowing for a bountiful and ongoing harvest of tasty young leaves.

---

### 🅐 Tomato 'Early Girl'
*Lycopersicon lycopercicum*

In the Great White North of Canada, 'Early Girl' is the queen of tomatoes. Not only does it produce tennis ball–sized fruit weeks earlier than most varieties (about 55 days), it tastes exceptional and yields the entire summer. It's an indeterminate, so you will need to give it a cage or similar support. Provide it a large container unless you are going to keep it pruned down. 'Early Girl' is resistant to fusarium wilt.

### **B** Viola 'Penny Mix'
Viola hybrids

This is the quintessential edible flower. Violas are small versions of pansies; they go by many names, and there are dozens of colours and sizes available. They are easy to grow from seed as long as they germinate in the dark. Shade them from the strong afternoon sun with larger edibles and don't be afraid to cut them back. The flowers have a mild wintergreen flavour and are usually used as decoration on cakes, either fresh or candied. Add the edible leaves to salads.

### **C** Chives
Allium schoenoprasum

see p. 171

### **D** Tomato 'Tumbler'
Lycopersicon lycopersicum

see p. 229

### **E** Lettuce 'Asian Baby Leaf'
Letuca sativa

see p. 213

### **F** Cucumber 'Pot Luck'
Cucumis sativus

'Pot Luck' is compact enough to be ideal for containers while still producing abundant fruit. It's a slicing cuke that yields 23 cm long fruit. The skin is prickly, so it's best peeled before eating. You can give 'Pot Luck' a trellis, but it is compact enough to use as a trailing plant (which is what I usually do). Give it plenty of fertilizer and don't let it dry out or you risk bitter fruit.

### **G** Parsley 'Triple Curled'
Petroselinum crispum

see p. 171

### **H** Rosemary 'Tuscan Blue'
Rosmarinus officinalis

see p. 217

# TEA PARTY

**Height:** to 1.5 m • **Spread:** to 1.5 m

**THIS RECIPE IS FOR PEOPLE** who take their tea as seriously as their gardening. You can easily make dozens of different teas with just the plants here, both in their pure forms and by mix-matching flavours.

**A** Tea plant

**B** Rose 'Hansa'

**C** Peppermint

**D** Lemon balm

**E** Strawberry 'Tristar'

**Recommended container size:**
80 cm across

Rose hips are the fruit of the rose that appear after blooming in spring but don't ripen to their rich rusty red colour until late summer. They contain plenty of lycopene and are one of the highest plant sources of vitamin C available. You can eat them raw if you don't mind the abrasive hairs, but most people prefer making tea.

*Rosa rugosa* hips are considered the best for culinary use. Harvest them after the first frost (which intensifies their flavour) and cut off both ends. Cut them in half, remove the seeds and wash the hips well. Dry them for a couple of days and you can make tea anytime you want by steeping and straining at will. Add dried lemon balm or peppermint leaves if you want some extra flavour.

Lemon balm is a deliciously scented mint that makes a soothing tea known to help with stomach pains and headaches. You can use fresh or dried leaves (I encourage you to experiment with both), about a heaping tea-spoon per boiling cup of water. Add honey or sugar to taste and enjoy.

As an edible gardener, you're growing roses for their hips; the flowers are a delighful bonus. 'Hansa' roses produce some of the biggest and best hips of any rose.

The peppermint is easy to grow and, being a mint, grows so fast that a few plants will provide ample tea leaves. To make tea, harvest the leaves, preferably in the morning, then rip them into small pieces and let them dry until they're crunchy (24 to 48 hours). Steep about one teaspoon per cup. Try not to consume more than one cup of peppermint tea a day.

Herbal infusions made from strawberry leaves can be a homemade remedy for diarrhea and even headaches.

Coffee makes an ideal houseplant in winter and, after a few years, will actually grow beans.

Use young, home-grown, healthy leaves. You don't need to dry them; simply steep them in boiling water. If the tisane gives you any stomach pain, stop drinking it.

## Making Your Own Black Tea

Tea is the second most widely consumed beverage in the world. It's remarkable that so many varieties of tea come from a nondescript *Camellia* plant. Each kind of tea made from the plant requires its own process and, as you might guess, you can choose how time-consuming you want the process to be. Here's the quickest way to make black tea.

Wait until your tea plant is large enough that it can sustain several handfuls of leaves being harvested. It has been known to live for over 1000 years, so no hurry. Harvest in spring, as the plant is coming out of dormancy. The fresh leaves taste the best and have about four percent caffeine. Snip (don't yank) newly grown twigs with two to three young leaves attached.

Spearmint tea is a classic herbal remedy for stomachache and insomnia, as well as being a potent antioxident.

Roll and crush the leaves under a rolling pin until they start to turn red, then spread them out on a tray (muslin cloth is the traditional way) and leave them in a cool place for two to three days. Once they've dried, bake them at 250° F for 20 minutes.

I want to stress that this is one way to make tea, but there are many more. Once you've made a few batches, start to be creative and try other kinds or even add flavourings.

---

### 🅐 Tea plant
*Camellia sinensis*

If you're serious about growing your own tea, this is the plant you need. Indigenous to China but now cultivated around the world, it's a one-stop tea shop, producing leaves for white tea, black tea, oolong tea and green tea. Bring it indoors in winter and it will give tea for generations. I suggest finding one online or at a large garden centre.

### 🅑 Rose 'Hansa'
*Rosa rugosa*

On the Prairies, where tea roses are usually annuals and options for hardy roses are scarce, 'Hansa' is the monarch of roses. It's an old-fashioned type that forms large shrubs with dark pink, 5 cm wide flowers that bloom all summer long. You may need to cut out the suckers. Rugosa hips are considered among the most flavourful of all roses.

### 🅒 Peppermint
*Mentha* x *piperita*

see p. 62

### 🅓 Lemon balm
*Melissa officinalis*

Harvested for over 2000 years for its antibacterial healing properties, this member of the mint family is a delight to the senses. Its leaves are dark green and coarse and release a sweet lemony smell when touched. In warmer climates I suggest keeping it in containers; it's as invasive as the other mints are. It's great in teas or candied with desserts.

### 🅔 Strawberry 'Tristar'
*Fragaria* hybrids

see p. 208

# PIZZA TONIGHT

**Height:** to 1 m • **Spread:** to 70 cm

**EVEN THOUGH PIZZA IS ONE** of the most popular meals in Canada, we rarely taste it the way it was meant to be tasted. As the heavily processed tastes of barbecue chicken and donair pizzas become the norm, they tend to make us forget that the original pizza from Naples relied on simple, fresh tomatoes, basil and olive oil for its exceptional taste. By growing the key ingredients yourself, you can fall in love with pizza all over again.

**A** Tomato 'Roma'

**B** Tomato 'Tumbling Tom Red'

**C** Tomato 'Tumbling Tom Yellow'

**D** Bell pepper 'Green Bell'

**E** English thyme

**F** Greek oregano

**G** Basil

**Recommended container size:** 45–60 cm across (2×) / 20–30 cm across

This recipe has everything you need, except the dough and cheese, to make an authentic Napolese pizza that is both far healthier and tastier than delivery (and you don't need to shell out a tip).

I used 'Roma' tomatoes because they are the most ubiquitous plum type and are easy to grow. If you're a purist, call around for 'San Marzano' tomatoes, which are native to the Napolese region and are, by some chefs' reckoning, the best-tasting in the world. You may have to order them online.

Fresh basil leaves bring a taste that can't be replicated. Pick young leaves just before you use them, being careful not to snip off more than a third of any stem. Whether you add basil to your pizza pie before or after baking is up to you. I add mine immediately after it comes out of the oven so that basil's leaves are warmed but not cooked; the flavour doesn't hold up well when baked. My wife often adds cherry tomatoes after baking, as well, for a juicier taste.

'Pesto' basil features dark green leaves and a zesty taste that's perfect for making pesto and pasta sauce.

If bell peppers aren't your favourite, consider substituting eggplant or, if you're a heat lover, some chilies. The tomatoes and basil will provide the classic pizza taste, and whatever you add after that is up to you.

## Making Fresh Tomato Sauce

The way we're used to making tomato sauce is to start with a can of crushed tomatoes. However, it's easy enough to make your own pizza sauce using home-grown tomatoes.

First, you'll need to pick a good amount of ripe tomatoes, making sure that they are uniformly red from top to bottom. If your vines don't provide enough, summer farmers' markets usually offer fresh Romas.

Plum types don't have many seeds and, unless you're fussy about one or two seeds, don't require straining. Cut them into small chunks. Again, unless you're fussy, I wouldn't bother skinning them; once you simmer, reduce and puree them there won't be much skin left to worry about.

You'll want to add fresh basil and oregano to your sauce. Cooking reduces basil's flavour, so be generous if you want to taste it. I didn't include garlic plants in this container because, though most sauce recipes call for it, it's a pain to grow in pots (involves winterizing) and is readily available fresh at farmers' markets.

'Roma' tomatoes will need some vertical support to grow well. They're ideal for making any kind of Italian dish.

### Ⓐ Tomato 'Roma'
*Lycopersicon lycopersicum*

see p. 93

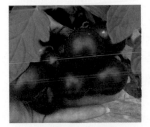

### Ⓑ Tomato 'Tumbling Tom Red'
*Lycopersicon lycopersicum*

Very similar to 'Tumbler' tomato, 'Tumbling Tom' is almost as bountiful and, in my opinion, healthier and more vigorous longer into the season. The fruit is tiny but you can expect 1–1.5 kg or more of it. Give it plenty of room because it gets larger than 'Tumbler,' but, being determinate, it won't need staking and is ideal for hanging baskets.

### Ⓒ Tomato 'Tumbling Tom Yellow'
*Lycopersicon lycopersicum*

Although a little less bountiful than its red counterpart, 'Tumbling Tom Yellow' will still yield lots of fruit on bushy, robust hanging plants. The fruit is sweet, yellow and gorgeous. Fertilize it often to keep it vigorous. I've found that 'Tumbling Tom' is much less vulnerable to crippling transplant shock than 'Tumbler.' It matures in a rapid 60–65 days.

### Ⓓ Bell pepper 'Green Bell'
*Capsicum annuum*

see p. 159

### Ⓔ English thyme
*Thymus vulgaris*

see p. 209

### Ⓕ Greek oregano
*Origanum vulgare* var. *hirtum*

see p. 102

### Ⓖ Basil
*Ocimum basilicum;* sweet basil

This quintessential Italian herb has varieties in warm regions across the globe and has found its way into countless dishes. Give it a warm, protected spot, well-drained soil and try to avoid fungal disease by not watering the leaves at night. Serve the tasty young leaves fresh because cooking dilutes the flavour.

# FRUIT SALAD

**Height:** to 70 cm • **Spread:** to 70 cm

**THIS RECIPE TAKES GRAZING** to a whole new level. Imagine grabbing blueberries and citrus right off the patio. Push your comfort zone of edible container plants by trying fruit and herb varieties that go way beyond beans and basil. By learning a few simple skills, like winterizing containers, the options and the sweet bounty go up exponentially.

**A** Blueberry 'Chippewa'

**B** Strawberry 'Berries Galore'

**C** Rhubarb 'Canada Red'

**D** Pineapple sage

**E** Stevia

**F** Lemon balm

**G** Apple mint

**H** Kumquat 'Nagami'

**Recommended container size:** 30 cm by 60 cm / 30 cm by 90 cm

This was a fun combination to put together because it allowed me to explore ingredients within a theme, in this case anything fruity, without being tied down to traditional edible ingredients. When you're designing your own containers, whether they have one ingredient or several, remember that having fun and trying new things is what this is all about.

From sweet berries and sugary leaves to tart stems, these pots are made for grazing. You can also have a lot of fun playing with the contents; whether it's making rhubarb pie or adding apple mint to ice cream, there are a lot of options here and they're all a bit outside the box.

Strawberries are the easiest and most rewarding fruit to grow in containers.

Hardy kiwis are smaller than the commercially available fuzzy kind, but are still sweet with edible skin and much hardier.

'Sugar Baby' watermelon's short maturity time makes it ideal for Canadian gardens. It isn't as big as supermarket watermelons, but so much sweeter.

By putting blueberries and strawberries in the same pot, I cheated on the pH for both of them a little. While the lower tolerance of strawberries is 5.5 and blueberries' upper tolerance is 5.0, I planted them in Canadian peat moss, which comes in at about 5.2. I opted for an ever-bearing strawberry because I wanted sweet berries all summer, not just in June.

The rhubarb is a personal favourite. Although it's not the hippest plant around, it's hardy and easy to grow and winterize. Because rhubarb's massive shape isn't great for pots, I kept one half of it pruned back to give room to the plants beside it. If rhubarb isn't your thing, consider some raspberry canes in a larger container. If you do use rhubarb, make sure that none of its poisonous leaves get mixed up with your herbs.

## Growing Blueberries in Pots

Blueberries are one of those plants that most people just assume can't be grown in pots. For many varieties, the opposite is true. However, though they are relatively easy to grow in pots, it can be hard to create a pocket of soil acidic enough for them without damaging nearby crops.

There are several different types of blueberry, from the 45 cm tall 'TopHat' to towering, 3 m tall highbush types. For containers, choose a dwarf type unless you're using a massive pot, like a half whiskey barrel, in which case you have your pick. The 'Chippewa' in my recipe tops out at 90 cm tall and is hardy on the Prairies. Make sure to have two, ideally three, blueberries close to each other for pollination.

You'll need a pH of 4.0–5.0. If you're willing to keep the hose handy straight peat moss is usually good enough, or you can use a blueberry/rhododendron mix that's readily available in warmer regions. Don't go too heavy with the fertilizer; organics and slow-release types are ideal for these light feeders.

Blueberries, like raspberries, don't really start paying off until they are a few years old. The first summer, the dozen berries you get will taste like heaven and you can look forward to many more. You'll need to winterize it, which sounds scary but is both easy and necessary in order to graduate to edible fruits in containers. I explain winterizing on pages 27–29. The larger the pot you have, the less work it'll be to prepare it for winter.

## Sunflowers

One of the best ways to turn your garden into a buffet is to plant sunflowers. When you think of sunflowers that produce edible seeds, probably the first varieties that come to mind are the monstrous 'Russian' and 'Titan' types that you need a ladder to harvest.

Recently, seed companies such as Renee's Garden have offered varieties that are easily grown in containers

and offer lots of fibre-rich, edible seeds. My favourite is 'Snack Seed.' It grows only about 1.5 m tall but produces disproportionately large heads with rows of seeds inside. Make sure it has ample sun and moisture.

Sunflowers are gorgeous in midsummer but then the petals die back, starting from the outside and moving to the centre as the tiny florets wither. Consider covering the head with

Blueberries take a few years to offer the big yields so the extra effort to winterize them is well worth it.

'Snack Seed' sunflower from Renee's Garden gives you, and the birds, a late season snack. You could also leave the heads on as a makeshift winter bird feeder.

a paper bag when this happens (pollination is taken care of by this point) so that the birds don't steal your crop.

Once the seeds are plump, pick them, dry them and enjoy them. You could also leave the seeds for the birds or even cut off the head and use it as a bird-feeder.

---

### A Blueberry 'Chippewa'

*Vaccinium corymbosum*

Hardy to zone 2, this half-highbush variety is one of the toughest around. Its compact size makes it ideal for containers, and it has striking fall colour. Overwinter it and in a few years it will produce a lot of berries. Use an acidic soil, like peat moss, and/or sprinkle spruce needles around it. Having more than one variety will increase your yield.

### B Strawberry 'Berries Galore'

*Fragaria* hybrids

see p. 213

### ⓒ Rhubarb 'Canada Red'
*Rheum rhabarbarum*

Although not an ideal container plant thanks to its width, with some regular pruning you can still enjoy rhubarb crumble and crisp without a garden. It's easy to grow in a large container and, if you keep it year after year, you can divide it and give the babies out to friends. 'Canada Red' has red stalks (called petioles) that keep their colour when cooked.

### Ⓓ Pineapple sage
*Salvia elegans*

see p. 213

### Ⓔ Stevia
*Stevia rebaudiana;* sweetleaf

Stevia is a South American native that has been used as a sweetener for centuries. It is now one of the most common sugar substitutes on supermarket shelves. It's difficult to grow from seed, so buy starter plants. Any temperature under 10° C shocks it, so wait for warm nights before planting it out. Try to use a fertilizer that's fairly low in nitrogen.

### Ⓕ Lemon balm
*Melissa officinalis*

see p. 123

### Ⓖ Apple mint
*Mentha suaveolens;* woolley mint

Apple mint is closely related to pineapple mint. Its cream-rimmed leaves make it a popular ornamental as well as a culinary addition. Use it to make apple mint jelly or mint tea, or you can use it as a garnish in salads and desserts. It grows to about 80 cm tall and prefers partial shade. It may be invasive, so keep it in a container.

### Ⓗ Kumquat 'Nagami'
*Citrus japonica*

These are delicious, olive-sized citrus fruits with a taste somewhere between a tangerine and a lime. Ideal for containers, they can be brought indoors in winter and will grow into a well-shaped tree with glossy, dark green foliage. Expect it to produce hundreds of fruit. The sweet, edible skin makes it an ideal patio-grazing edible, or if they're too tart, use them in marmalades.

# HEARTY FLAVOURS

**Height:** to 90 cm • **Spread:** to 70 cm

**WE USUALLY ASSOCIATE** growing our own food with long, summer days grazing in the garden and salads picked fresh that morning. This recipe looks forward to the shorter days of fall, when the kids are back in school and crisp patio lettuce is a memory. For those days, nothing beats a hearty soup.

Ⓐ Bay

Ⓑ Lemon grass

Ⓒ Onion 'Sweet Spanish'

Ⓓ Lovage

Ⓔ Carrots 'Nantes'

Ⓕ Celery 'Utah 52–70'

Ⓖ Leek

**Recommended container size:** 60 cm across

While this container doesn't have a lot of anything, it has some of a lot of things. If you have a favourite or two that you want to see here (beets for me), I suggest planting an extra pot beside this one.

Celery is a beneficial companion to tomatoes, cauliflower, cabbage and especially leeks. When celery is planted in the garden, earthworms love making homes in its lacy root system.

Celery has been reported to have a hypoglycemic effect and may be useful in treating Type 2 diabetes by lowering blood sugar levels. The leaves and seeds have also been found to help the body better use insulin. Before using any plant as a drug, however, it's best to chat with your doctor about potential side effects.

Leeks are always hungry and love a lot of organic matter in their soil.

They grow beneficially with celery and onions. Carrots also help their growth, and in return leeks keep away carrot flies.

With lovage being so beefy, it will need frequent pruning so it doesn't

Bay's slow growth makes it a powerfully impressive specimen plant once it gets large.

block out the much slower growing bay. Besides being a desirable habitat for beneficial predatory beetles, lovage increases the health and vitality of any plant it is paired with.

## Growing Carrots and Beets in Pots

A lot of people think that just because their edible bits grow below the soil and not above it, root vegetables can't be grown in containers. The reality is that carrots and beets are among the easiest plants to grow in pots.

Both of these are cool weather crops that thrive in spring and fall temperatures between 15° and 18° C. Plant them in airy, organic, peaty soil where their roots can grow and swell easily. They have some of the longest shelf lives of any home-grown veggies, so they are a great way to carry your vitamin intake forward into winter.

Weeds and poor drainage in the ground often hamper these crops, so containers provide ideal conditions. Direct seed them about 2.5 cm apart; you'll need to thin them later to about 5 cm apart. You can start early in containers because you don't have to wait for the soil to thaw. Make sure your container is at least 30 cm deep so the roots have room to grow.

When it comes to fertilizer, take it easy on the nitrogen. Too much of it can lead to hairy and fibrous roots. Sprinkling some wood ashes among your carrots is a great way to give them an extra dose of potassium.

Beets and carrots are mature when the top of the root is about 2.5 cm in diameter, though you can harvest before that. Be wary of letting them mature too long lest you get a tough crop. Don't panic about an early fall frost because you can harvest even after hard frosts.

Nothing beats the taste of fresh beets, newly pulled and boiled with butter.

Carrots are one of the most versatile veggies you can grow, and they take up very little space in a container.

### 🅐 Bay
*I aurus nobllis;* sweet bay

Grown from the beginning of recorded history, bay has a rich history. It's easy, albeit slow, to grow, and a large bay tree is a specimen that takes years to accomplish. Use the leaves to flavour soups, stocks and braises, though the leaves themselves aren't eaten. They accumulate flavour as they dry, so pick them a couple weeks before using.

### 🅑 Lemon grass
*Cymbopogon citratus*

see p. 71

### 🅒 Onion 'Sweet Spanish'
*Allium cepa*

see p. 86

### 🅓 Lovage
*Levisticum officinale*

see p. 182

### 🅔 Carrots 'Nantes'
*Daucus carota*

see p. 111

### 🅕 Celery 'Utah 52-70'
*Apium graveolens*

Probably the only food that you lose calories by eating it, celery is a healthy snack that does well in containers as long as it's kept well watered and the pot is at least 20 cm deep. It needs plenty of fertilizer and has a long growing season. 'Utah 52-70' is a popular variety, while 'Pascal' is the supermarket type. You can eat it fresh or use it in almost any cooked dish.

### 🅖 Leek
*Allium ampeloprasum* subsp. *porrum*

Leeks are tasty on their own or in stews and soups. They form a vertical, tightly bound shaft of leafy stalks. Grow them in 30 cm or deeper containers. You may want to overwinter them because they take so long to mature. Blanche them by leaving the soil level in the container low, then mounding it around the leek stems when they're near maturity.

# TINY HARVEST
## Sprouts

**Height:** N/A • **Spread:** N/A

**WHEN IT COMES TO EATING** healthy, the tiny sprout goes a long
way. Sprouts have more vitamins, nutrients and minerals than any
other food per calorie. As soon as you pour water on that humble
seed, its biochemical processes spring into action. It starts to create
vitamins B and C, and massive amounts of carotene, niacin and thia-
mine (depending on the type of seed, of course).

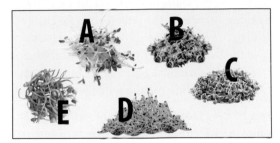

**A** Alfalfa

**B** Broccoli

**C** Lentil

**D** Onion

**E** Mung bean

**Recommended container size:** Mason jar

Sprouts have been used to fend off scurvy and as a vitamin supplement, grown in the trenches during wartime. They are perfect in winter because they are the anti-processed food. They are fresh, they are perishable and they have more vitamins and enzymes per gram than any other food.

Studies have even demonstrated that some types of sprouts, especially broccoli, can help protect blood cells and may reduce the risk of cancer and/or heart disease. Other sprouts, such as radish, alfalfa and clover, may also help prevent some cancers.

## Growing Sprouts in a Jar

The easiest method to grow sprouts is also the one that intimidates people the most: hydroponically. It sounds a lot more complex than it

Canning jars are an ideal place to grow sprouts, as long as you change the water daily.

actually is, so bear with me. It may seem like there are a lot of silly rules when growing sprouts, but it's all to keep the environment sterile and the food safe.

Different sprouts have different germinating times, but most are ready to eat in just a few days. The only materials you are going to need are some sprout seeds, a glass canning jar and some muslin or cheese cloth. You can user paper towels in a pinch.

Make sure the seed you are using is identified as seeds for sprouting. Don't go to the bird section for sunflower seeds or the bulk section for chick peas. These seeds have often been treated with various chemicals that will inhibit germination, causing some seeds to rot and spoil the whole batch.

Place a tablespoon of seeds in the jar. Don't put too many seeds in as they will expand dramatically. Swirl them in warm (not hot) water for about a minute, then drain the jar. Add more water until it is a couple inches above the seeds. Let them soak in a cool, dark spot for about 12 hours (longer for bigger seeds).

Bean sprouts are an Asian classic and essential in stir-fries and other Eastern dishes.

With the cheese cloth or strainer in place (secured by the outside of the lid or a sturdy elastic), tip the jar upside down to drain it, then lay the jar on its side to spread out the seeds. Keep it cool and out of direct light. Some people give the water used for soaking, which is full of nutrients, to their houseplants.

Two to three times a day, rinse your sprouts with water, swirling them gently so that the water doesn't break the tender shoots. Drain it after each rinse, making sure you get all the water out. The sprouts should stay moist but shouldn't sit in water; seeds left in standing water can rot and ruin the batch.

After a few days the sprouts will be filling the jar and they will be ready to eat. Check the seed package to see how long the sprouts should be to harvest. If you want the tips of the sprouts to green up, expose them to a few hours of light just before you pick them.

Rinse them well in a colander and store them loosely in an airtight bag. If you want to eat your sprouts over a period of time, putting them in the refrigerator will slow down their growth. They will usually keep for about a week if you rinse them every day or two to keep them moist.

Use your sprouts cooked or raw, on sandwiches, in salads or just on their own. The internet is a great resource for learning about the creative ways to use your sprouts now that you've grown them.

After your harvest you'll probably want to start over again. Once you get a system going, growing your own sprouts is easier, and a lot cheaper, than driving to the supermarket to buy them.

Pound for pound, sprouts are among the healthiest and most nutrient-rich edibles you can grow, and also one of the easiest.

## Health Concerns and Safe Practices

Imported sprouts have gotten some bad press lately thanks to a nasty little bug called *E. coli*. While it's true that sprouting seeds are more susceptible to bacterial growth, it's also true that if you use clean equipment there's no more danger than there is with any other raw food.

When you grow your own food you control the conditions, the procedure and the standards, which is another reason why I recommend growing sprouts over buying them. Here are a few tips to make sure your harvests are safe and healthy.

- Start with clean equipment, making sure to wash it if it's new or in between uses.

- Use glass jars over plastic; I recommend Mason jars.

- Rinse your seeds before soaking them, and use filtered water if your water supply is questionable.

- Keep the sprouts away from direct light and in a cool place to inhibit bacterial growth.

The important thing is that you keep the growing environment sterile. Wash your hands before and after you handle the seeds/sprouts, and if you notice mould or a bad smell emanating from the jar, you should toss the whole batch, sterilize everything and start again. Don't be afraid to be over-cautious; it's better safe than sorry.

Not every vegetable makes a good sprout. Members of the potato family (including tomatoes, peppers and eggplants) are poisonous as sprouts.

You can grow sprouts in soil as long as you wash them very well before eating.

### Ⓐ Alfalfa
*Medicago sativa*

This classic sandwich sprout is easy, has a satisfying crunch and is packed with vitamins. While it's ubiquitous in stores, it's worth growing for its refreshing, mild taste and its link to the prevention of cancer and heart disease. It's great in omelettes. The seeds expand to about seven times their volume in the five to six days it takes to sprout.

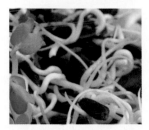

### Ⓑ Broccoli
*Brassica oleracea* var. *botrytis*

Broccoli is the sprout most closely linked to cancer prevention. When we eat the young plant, we're also eating the antioxidant chemicals that the plant uses to protect itself. Broccoli goes from seed to sprout in three to six days, and the finished sprout is about five times the volume of the seed. It has a mild peppery taste.

### Ⓒ Lentil
*Lens culinaris*

Humans have been eating this legume since neolithic times. The large, yellow seeds are quick to sprout (two to three days), and the light green sprouts have lots of protein and plenty of vitamins A, B and C as well as calcium. I recommend lentil sprouts in Asian cuisine, especially stir-fries. They expand to about twice the volume as the seeds.

### Ⓓ Onion
*Allium cepa*

While most sprouts are roots, onion sprouts are shoots and have a tangy flavour reminiscent of the adult version. They fit in wherever you want a subtle but not overpowering onion taste. Onion shoots are a great source of vitamins A, C and D, as well as protein. They take longer to sprout, about two weeks, at which point the sprouts are five times the seed volume. They have beautiful black ends on them.

### Ⓔ Mung bean
*Vigna radiata*

These are the most consumed sprout on earth, especially in Asia where they are typically eaten raw just as we eat alfalfa sprouts raw in the West. They're rich in vitamins B, C and E, as well as calcium, amino acids and proteins. The creamy, fat sprouts take three to five days to grow and expand to two to three times the volume of the seed.

# BOLD AND TASTY
## Exploring Red

**Height:** to 80 cm · **Spread:** to 60 cm

**RED IS THE COLOUR** of passion, danger and boldness. If you have red in your garden it will stand out like a stop sign and always draw the eye. It's a colour that cries out to be seen and, when you create a red design with edibles, it will be that much more powerful.

**A** Bell pepper 'Cute Stuff Red'

**B** Lettuce 'Sea of Red'

**C** Nasturtium 'Empress of India'

**D** Tomato 'Tumbler'

**E** Strawberry 'Berries Galore'

**F** Beets 'Red Ace'

**Recommended container size:**
30–40 cm across

From roots to leaves to fruit, you have to think outside the flower when colour blocking with edibles. With annual container gardening, flowers steer the look of the entire composition. The secret to creating beautiful designs with edibles is to know that, though you're not going to get the same blast of colour that dahlias and petunias bring, you have other design elements that you can explore and be creative with.

I chose a 'Cute Stuff' bell pepper as my centrepiece because I'm a sucker for peppers' glossy texture. 'Cute Stuff Red' boasts small peppers that, though they are just a little more than bite-sized, produce vigorously in the summer heat. You could easily substitute an 'Early Girl' or even 'Roma' tomato, but you'd need a bigger pot and perhaps larger surrounding plants to match the change of scale.

Red is bold and potent no matter the shade, and when paired with green it creates a raucous contrast in the garden.

For the filler elements, I opted for foliage over fruit. 'Sea of Red' lettuce is a deliciously translucent red that shimmers when the sun hits it. It will bolt in the summer scorch, so keep fresh seed handy. Beets, one of my favourites, infuse robust warmth.

Red is one of the few colours that you have ample choice for trailing elements, so I took advantage and planted strawberries and 'Tumbler' tomatoes to round out the composition.

Edible flowers are the best way to add colour. The 'Empress of India' nasturtium is a classic that's easy to grow and brings red-stained leaves and vibrant scarlet flowers to the party. Being among the easiest and cheapest flowers to grow (throw the seeds in the dirt), no edible patio garden should be without them. Seed companies such as Renee's Garden offer dozens of varieties so you can accurately plan your colour schemes.

## Designing with Warm Colours

Warm colours are rich, deep, invigorating colours such as reds, bronzes and pinks—colours that catch the sun and glow as if they could heat up a living room in winter. They seem to come close to you when you look at them, as if they are walking to you or you are being drawn in to them. This illusion makes warm colours very intimate and personal.

Colour doesn't distinguish between edibles and annuals. Whether it's the red of a tomato or a verbena, the boldness and warmth will radiate out just the same. Don't hesitate to position edible containers in with annuals. For that matter, if edible flowers don't bring the wow factor you're looking for, you can blend annuals right in with your beets and lettuce. Just make sure you eat the right ones.

Warm colours always seem to be advancing toward the viewer, making them more intimate than cool colours.

### A Bell pepper 'Cute Stuff Red'

*Capsicum annuum;* sweet pepper

This prolific little character is the most compact bell pepper around. In about 55 days it produces ripe, red peppers. Although they are only about the size of an apricot (to start, anyway), the plant produces a surprising amount of them, making the starter plant a worthy investment. This is just one of the many varieties of compact veggies made for containers that is about to hit the market.

### B Lettuce 'Sea of Red'

*Letuca sativa*

First grown by the ancient Egyptians, lettuce is an easy-to-grow crop that thrives in the cool weather of spring and fall. 'Sea of Red' is a leaf type from Renee's Garden, so you can harvest a little and harvest often. The deep red, crinkled leaves have a mild, buttery flavour and aren't bitter unless they get too hot. They are best enjoyed fresh in colourful salads.

### C Nasturtium 'Empress of India'

*Tropaeolum majus*

see p. 171

### D Tomato 'Tumbler'

*Lycopersicon lycopersicum*

see p. 229

### E Strawberry 'Berries Galore'

*Fragaria* hybrids

see p. 213

### F Beets 'Red Ace'

*Beta vulgaris*

Beets are one of my favourite vegetables. The colour of the blood red flesh is intoxicating when you cut into it, and fresh beets, peeled and cooked with a little butter, taste incredible. 'Red Ace' is a sweet variety that matures quickly and is ideal for Canadian patios. Beets love cool weather and will thrive in spring and fall. Make sure your container is at least 30 cm deep.

# THE ROYAL GARDEN
## Exploring Purple

**Height:** to 80 cm • **Spread:** to 60 cm

**PURPLE IS A MOODY COLOUR** that changes with the light. At noon it's bright and vibrant, but by dusk it's brooding and mysterious. It's also one of the most interesting colours to design with because it's always full of surprises. Try pairing it with the yellow design (see p. 152) for an exuberant blast of contrast.

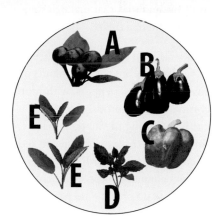

**A** Ornamental pepper 'Black Pearl'

**B** Eggplant 'Pot Black'

**C** Bell pepper 'Purple Beauty'

**D** Basil 'Purple'

**E** Purple sage

**Recommended container size:**
45–60 cm across

I thought that colour blocking edibles would be frustrating because there are far fewer options than with annuals, but on the contrary it was refreshing. Every spring I see people standing among the annuals at the greenhouse, seemingly shell-shocked at the sheer number of varieties available. With edibles, if you have a colour scheme in mind there are so few ingredients that a container almost builds itself.

The textures in this one make it my favourite of the four colour-blocked recipes. From the glossy peppers and basil to the soft sage and eggplant leaves, these edibles offer a lot more than just colour.

'Purple Beauty' pepper was my first choice for a compact yet colourful focal point. You could also use 'Field of Dreams' ornamental corn, which is a relatively new introduction with vividly striped leaves. It's not edible, but the birds love it.

Fuchsia, like the one here at Rideau Hall in Ottawa, is not only gorgeous but also produces edible berries.

The 'Pot Black' eggplant is a marvel. As if the delicate, papery flowers weren't enough, it follows up by yielding up to eight eggplants at a time on a bafflingly compact plant.

Purple trailing edibles are hard to come by, so I let my basil grow large enough that it flopped over the side. Hot weather will help make your basil branch out and stay bushy. Make sure to pinch off the flowers as they bud, and don't harvest too much stem at any one time. The same goes for the purple sage, which has about the same flavour as the green variety.

## Designing with Peppers

The amazing thing about peppers is that just when you think you've seen them all, you find out you haven't. The variety is endless, and they have multiple qualities that make designing with them a treat.

Let's start with colour. From purple to yellow, you can get your hands on a rainbow of bell peppers, with more compact and vigorously blooming cultivars hitting the market all the time. Whether it's the fire-alarm red of cayenne peppers or the slick yellow of banana peppers, every colour is vibrant and bright—no pastels or soft earth tones here.

Peppers come in a variety of textures, from bulging bells to glossy, smooth jalapenos to wrinkled, almost violent-looking habaneros with their lurking intensity. We can feel textures long before we actually touch them, so while the bells will invite you closer, habaneros are a warning.

There is a universe of shapes, colours and even textures of peppers available, especially if you grow them from seed.

There are even unique shapes. Thai chilies curve like devilish scimitars while cherry peppers are as round as tomatoes, and habaneros resemble Chinese lanterns.

---

### Ⓐ Ornamental pepper 'Black Pearl'
*Capsicum annuum*

I love the textures here. This exceptionally beautiful pepper is sold as an ornamental for its layers of glossy, delectably dark purple leaves and clusters of olive-sized peppers with an almost mirror finish. The peppers ripen to red, and while they are edible they are extremely hot; don't approach if you're not used to heat. Keep the plant year after year as a houseplant.

### Ⓑ Eggplant 'Pot Black'
*Solanum melongena;* aubergine

Eggplants are heat lovers that are as easy to grow as peppers. 'Pot Black' is a wonderful miniature variety that produces handfuls of tennis ball–sized fruit. You can let them hang on the vine for a unique texture and colour, but harvest when they're still glossy. The fruit is bitter when raw but develops a complex taste when cooked.

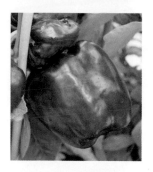

### Ⓒ Bell pepper 'Purple Beauty'
*Capsicum annuum;* sweet pepper

The rainbow of bell peppers gets broader with this relatively new introduction. Stocky, compact plants produce small peppers at first, but with enough heat the larger root system will give you fist-sized fruit so heavy it drags down the plant. The peppers are sweet with a thick skin, and they make a beautiful addition to salads and stir-fries. As with all peppers, find any trick in the book to provide this one with extra heat and direct sun.

### Ⓓ Basil 'Purple'
*Ocimum basilicum*

see p. 221

### Ⓔ Purple sage
*Salvia officinalis* 'Purpurascens'

see p. 163

# SUNDROP
## Exploring Yellow

**Height:** to 80 cm • **Spread:** to 60 cm

**YELLOW IS THE COLOUR** of pure, honest joy and brings beauty everywhere it goes. In the garden, it's like a refreshing glass of lemonade when placed among the heavy drama of reds and purples. Although yellow edible options are limited, there are still enough to make your design shine.

- **A** Bell pepper 'Golden Summer'
- **B** Banana pepper 'Sweet Banana'
- **C** Calendula 'Bon Bon Mix'
- **D** Pineapple mint
- **E** Tomato 'Tumbling Tom Yellow'
- **F** Lemon grass

**Recommended container size:**
45–60 cm across

As with the other colours, peppers were the easy choice for a focal point. You could substitute 'Lemon Boy' tomatoes if you switched to a larger pot size or even use another yellow cherry tomato, such as 'Sungold.' I opted for both a banana pepper and a bell pepper.

I added lemon grass as filler because it brings a stirring architectural touch. It's technically a cheat because it's not yellow, but I rationalized that the word "lemon" qualified it for this design.

There's an ongoing debate about whether 'Tumbling Tom' or 'Tumbler' is the better value for cherry tomatoes. 'Tumbler' has better word-of-mouth, and while countless people come in every year looking for it, I prefer 'Tumbling Tom.' It takes a little longer to yield, but its habit is fuller and its foliage is healthier than its more popular cousin.

No matter what colour scheme your design is, chances are there's a bell pepper to go with it; perhaps these 'Golden Bells.'

I love pineapple mint in drinks and with desserts. Its creamy variegation and playful texture are ideal additions here. The catch is that you'll get more leaves than you could ever use.

Calendula is an under-appreciated marvel. Often dismissed as a cottage flower, it's finding new life and well-deserved appreciation as a "retro" edible flower that, when it comes to flower power, out-performs almost anything else in the edible garden. Deadhead spent blossoms, and more will take their place.

## Designing with Tomatoes

Think you know tomatoes? I did, until I started learning about the staggering array of colours, shapes and sizes available. The grow-your-own movement has brought a surge of interest in heirloom plant varieties (an heirloom is an original, non-hybridized variety). Heirloom tomatoes push the limits of how we define the round, red fruit we all know. However, many of the unique heirloom varieties have such long maturation times that you'll rarely see the fruit.

I'm a sucker for the classic glossy red salad tomatoes like 'Early Girl,' but there is a huge variety of colours and sizes available. The more popular varieties, like red or yellow cherry tomatoes, will almost always have fruit ripe on the vine, which makes them a potent design element. Cherry tomatoes are small (bite-sized) and grow along stems on the vine. The cluster creates eye-catching architecture. Grape tomatoes are even smaller and form longer, denser clusters.

While tomato plants aren't known for having a pleasingly aesthetic shape, you can train indeterminates so the vines grow however you like. Types such as 'Sungold' form long, pendulous stems that can be tied, braced or trellised into intriguing architectural patterns.

Cherry tomatoes bear so much fruit that you can reliably incorporate the fruits' colour into your design scheme.

### Ⓐ Bell pepper 'Golden Summer'
*Capsicum annuum;* sweet pepper

'Golden Summer' produces blocky fruit that start green and ripen to golden yellow. The fruit is exceptionally sweet, which makes it excellent for eating right off the plant or chopped into a fresh and colourful summer salad. Its tendency for a short season makes it ideal for Canada. In warmer regions, pinch off the early flowers to get more foliage and bigger peppers in the long run.

### Ⓑ Banana pepper 'Sweet Banana'
*Capsicum annuum*

Banana peppers are one of the easiest types of peppers to grow and produce sweet, 8 cm long, yellow fruit. They have almost no heat, and you can harvest them when they are full size and the skin becomes firm. They're perfect for dieters because they have very low calorie, fat and sodium levels. They add a sweet tang either raw in salads or cooked in almost anything.

### Ⓒ Calendula 'Bon Bon Mix'
*Calendula officinalis*

see p. 110

### Ⓓ Pineapple mint
*Mentha suaveolens* 'Variegata'

Like most other flavoured mints, this one lives up to its billing by bringing a sweet pineapple scent and taste to containers. It's also one of the prettiest mints, bringing some cream variegation and fuzzy texture to the bunch. Being low growing and not quite as pushy as its cousins, it makes a great ornamental plant as well as a herb. Provide it some shelter from the afternoon scorch and keep it well watered.

### Ⓔ Tomato 'Tumbling Tom Yellow'
*Lycopersicon lycopersicum*

see p. 127

### Ⓕ Lemon grass
*Cymbopogon citratus*

see p. 71

# THE DEEP WOODS
## Exploring Green

**Height:** to 80 cm • **Spread:** to 60 cm

**CONTAINER GARDENING HAS BECOME** obsessed with colour. In this recipe, form and texture leap out of the pot because, in the absence of other colours, we can take a deep breath and appreciate the rich complexity and the wonder that green brings.

**A** Bell pepper 'Green Bell'

**B** Rosemary 'Tuscan Blue'

**C** Habanero pepper

**D** Chives

**E** Parsley 'Triple Curled'

**F** Greek oregano

**G** Curly-leaved kale

**Recommended container size:** 45– 60 cm across

We often take green for granted. It's the anchoring colour in the garden, typically dismissed as a background set piece for the colourful prima donnas in the spotlight. It's only when we're confronted with nothing but green that we realize it is probably the most complex and enigmatic colour in the spectrum.

Green is both the colour of fresh, young, healthy life and of decaying sickness. Seedlings are bright green as they emerge into a new world, and mould is green as it layers and rots. With a colour this paradoxical, the design potential is endless.

I celebrated shapes in this recipe. The kale is an aesthetic superstar that dominates the composition with its tantalizing shapes. Kale is also intensely healthy and one of the tastier and more versatile ingredients here.

Chives add architectural appeal with their dense vertical lines. If you want to emphasize the vertical aspect, plant onions; though less dense, they're fatter and won't fall over as easily. When designing with edibles, pounce on any straight lines you can because they are few and far between. Rosemary offers a host of tiny straight lines jutting off in every direction.

'Tuscan' kale is a staple in traditional Italian dishes like minestrone.

When it comes to design, few edibles rival 'Triple Curled' parsley. It grows into a bell-shaped mass of jagged edges and folds. The oregano isn't much for form, but its fuzzy, button-shaped leaves bring a textural contrast.

I chose green bell peppers knowing that I wouldn't be able to let them fully ripen unless I wanted a red visitor to the mix. A green bell pepper is simply one that has been picked before it fully ripened into colour. I added a habanero because I like its shape. Its fruit will be orange, but they take so long to arrive that they won't affect the colour scheme.

Designing with green makes the textures of the ingredients spring to life. Don't be afraid to mix them up.

## Designing with Cool Colours

On the other side of the palette from warm colours are the cool colours such as silvers, blues and greens. Cool colours seem to recede from us when we look at them; a garden full of cool designs can look serene and refreshing, but it can also seem as far away as the crisp blue sky.

In edibles, green is the dominant cool colour, though you can also find blue- and silver-tinged leaves on herbs and vegetables. Cool designs tend to have a more subtle interplay of colours than warm designs. Cool-coloured plants also tend to boast more architectural appeal than their warm-coloured, braggart counterparts. What cool schemes lack in audacity, they make up for in curiosity.

Cool, crisp colours like silver and light green create an invigorating container that is energizing to look at.

### Ⓐ Bell pepper 'Green Bell'

*Capsicum annuum;* sweet pepper

All bell peppers start green and ripen into an ever-broadening rainbow of cultivars. You can use green peppers fresh in salads, cooked in stir-fries or barbecued with other veggies or meats. They're easy to grow as long as they have plenty of heat. Don't expect supermarket-sized fruit, but they will get larger as the plant does.

### Ⓑ Rosemary 'Tuscan Blue'

*Rosmarinus officinalis*

see p. 217

### Ⓒ Habanero pepper

*Capsicum chinense*

Native to the Amazon, this little pepper looks innocent but is the hottest naturally occurring pepper on the planet; it needs to be approached with caution. Add it to any dish you want to make borderline unbearable. Give it lots of heat and watch nervously as the 5 cm long peppers ripen to orange. If you bring it indoors over winter it will get quite large.

### Ⓓ Chives

*Allium schoenoprasum*

see p. 171

### Ⓔ Parsley 'Triple Curled'

*Petroselinum crispum*

see p. 171

### Ⓕ Greek oregano

*Origanum vulgare* var. *hirtum*

see p. 102

### Ⓖ Curly-leaved kale

*Brassica oleracea* var. *acephala*

Kale is a non-heading type of cabbage that thrives in containers and loves cool spring and fall temperatures, which intensify its flavour and colour. It's easy to grow and is loaded with vitamins and nutrients. From a design perspective, the texture that curly-leaved kale brings to containers is irresistible. There are red and purple varieties as well.

# KALEIDOSCOPE WINDOW

**Height:** to 70 cm • **Spread:** to 90 cm

**THIS RECIPE IS A KALEIDOSCOPIC** demonstration of the array of shapes available for an edible garden. From straight lines to crisp circles and plumes of texture, this design proves that you can give the eyes an aesthetic feast without relying on colour. I hope you get some ideas here about the stunning possibilities of mixing shapes.

**A** Rosemary 'Tuscan Blue'

**B** Nasturtium 'Whirlybird Mix'

**C** Curly willow

**D** Corn 'Field of Dreams'

**E** Fennel

**F** Chives

**G** Pansy 'Majestic Giants Mix'

**H** Swiss chard 'Bright Lights'

**I** Purple sage

**J** Strawberry 'Berries Galore'

**Recommended container size:** 30 cm by 75 cm

The show-stopping contrast here is between the thin, vertically branching rosemary stems and the broad, sand-dollar shaped nasturtium leaves. They radiate energy off each other.

Behind these are curly willow, fennel and the new 'Field of Dreams' ornamental corn for vertical appeal. Besides onions and lemon grass, it's hard to find bold architectural elements in the edibles world. The curly willow, though not edible, adds a strong dose of vertical scale. You could easily make curly willow into a trellis, as I did in several other designs, by planting a vining plant at its base.

The chives are a smaller vertical element that helps bring the eye down from the willow to the base of the window box. Just as our eyes follow similar colours, while enclosing the space between them, so too do they follow similar shapes and textures. You can guide the eye around your container by planting similar shapes that flow out of and into each other.

To even things out, we added several bunching plants in the front. Swiss chard, pansies and purple sage add texture and a strong dose of colour.

Strawberries and nasturtiums flow over the sides and help to mask the window box. You might have to be creative with edible trailers and look to plants that "flop" as well as deliberately trail, like nasturtiums.

## Window Box Design

They fell out of fashion for a long time, but now window boxes are being rediscovered and are on the way to becoming more popular than they've ever been. Because of their long,

Rosemary and nasturtiums have radically different textures and shapes, which makes them energizing when paired together.

narrow shape, it's easy to make them seem larger than they really are.

The secret to giving the appearance of extra depth to a window box is to plant three layers of ingredients into the narrow space. For the back, choose plants—such as corn and fennel—that are tall enough to make a statement but not so wide that they take up much space. Then plant a layer of wide, full plants as filler. The beefier the better to give the illusion of a large scale and make the tall rear plants look bigger.

You probably won't have much soil space left for the front row, so choose plants that don't take up much room at soil level but billow generously over the side. Nasturtiums are ideal because they grow wherever there's an open space to move into.

### Ⓐ Rosemary 'Tuscan Blue'
*Rosmarinus officinalis*

see p. 217

### Ⓑ Nasturtium 'Whirlybird Mix'
*Tropaeolum majus*

see p. 171

### Ⓒ Curly willow
*Salix matsudana*

Although not edible, curly willow brings both exotic, twisting lines and a potentially very versatile tool to your containers. The branches are cut from corkscrew willow trees and are typically sold only at Christmas, so you may need to store them. If you keep fresh stems in water they will often leaf out and even grow roots.

### ⓓ Corn 'Field of Dreams'
*Zea mays*

Although it's not an edible variety, I included 'Field of Dreams' corn because aesthetically pleasing centrepieces are hard to come by in the edibles world. It's a new variety that features rose-coloured variegation and a vigorous habit. Birds seem to love the seeds, but while some people say you can pop them, I'm skeptical. Leave it in the container over winter for some architecture appeal in your snowy yard.

### ⓔ Fennel
*Foeniculum vulgare*

see p. 78

### ⓕ Chives
*Allium schoenoprasum*

see p. 171

### ⓖ Pansy 'Majestic Giants Mix'
*Viola* x *wittrockiana*

see p. 167

### ⓗ Swiss chard 'Bright Lights'
*Beta vulgaris* subsp. *cicla*

see p. 225

### ⓘ Purple sage
*Salvia officinalis* 'Purpurascens'

Purple sage tastes slightly more muted than its green counterpart, and it is often used more as an ornamental. It brings a rugged texture, along with a captivatingly rich colour, to containers. Pinch it often and it will grow into a beautifully formed plant. Use it just as you would use garden sage, or as a cut flower.

### ⓙ Strawberry 'Berries Galore'
*Fragaria* hybrids

see p. 213

# PANSY PERFECT

**Height:** to 60 cm • **Spread:** to 60 cm  /

**IN CONTRAST WITH THE CHARTREUSE** buoyancy of the nasturtium mix (see p. 168), this design effectively, and subtly, uses purple and dark green to create a stability that anchors it and, though not heavy to the point of menacing, makes it appear heavier than it is. It would be an eye-catching complement to the vivacious nasturtiums.

**A** Pansy 'Majestic Giants Mix'

**B** Kale 'Pigeon Red'

**C** Tomato 'Patio'

**D** Fennel

**E** Parsley 'Triple Curled'

**Recommended container size:** 30–40 cm across

I'm a sucker for pansies. Not only are they curiously expressive, but they also have multiple personalities thanks to the vast repertoire of colours available. Normally we associate pansies with the broad, black grins splashed across sunlight yellow petals. Here, a much darker pansy conveys a different mood altogether, one with more gravitas and thoughtfulness.

The Salisbury production team put this one together. They used a tomato instead of a pepper because, unlike the optimistic gloss of the pepper, tomatoes have a darker, textured leaf that grounds the eye. They chose the well-behaved, determinate 'Patio' tomato because it thrives in small containers and doesn't need staking.

They used an ornamental kale because it's more compact than other varieties. Although it's usually not indicated on the label, ornamental kale is as edible as any other variety. As with any plant that garden centres don't normally treat as food, it's best to grow your own from seed in case it has been sprayed or treated.

Fennel is the comic relief here and livens up the dark greens and broad,

The cool greens of sage and chives, along with the container, blend in here with the vivid colours of the pansies.

heavy leaves with light-hearted, upward-flowing, ferny stems. You can use the herbal or the vegetable variety, though if you use the veggie fennel (called Florence fennel), you may need a bigger pot.

This pot is great for either grazing or a summery snack; sprinkle parsley and a little vinegar over the salad tomatoes.

## Making Candied Pansies

When it comes to pansies, you can choose from an array of colours, sizes and even textures. They will thrive in spring and fall, but they will probably wilt in the midsummer heat, especially if they don't have adequate afternoon shade. They will bounce back in fall if you don't push

them in July. Keep the soil moist, snip them back lightly and provide ample fertilizer.

Candied pansies were popular in Victorian England, and gardeners and bakers alike are rediscovering them today. They are an ideal addition to wedding cakes, cupcakes and ice cream, and they're surprisingly easy to make.

Pick as many fresh pansies as you want and wash and dry them well. Large, brightly coloured flowers typically make the biggest impact. Try to snip off the unpalatable stems.

Whisk an egg white with a few drops of water in a bowl until bubbles appear. Some people use gelatin instead of an egg. Gently brush the mixture onto the flower with a small

Ruffled pansies, also called whiskered pansies, add an edible twist wherever they are.

paintbrush. You want enough to coat the entire flower but not so much that it's dripping off.

Sprinkle both sides with a fine coating of sugar and put them on a sheet of wax paper to dry.

### Ⓐ Pansy 'Majestic Giants Mix'
*Viola* x *wittrockiana*

I'm probably not supposed to pick favourites, but pansies are my favourite. Beautiful, cheerful and easy to grow, they are the quintessential edible flower. 'Majestic Giants' is the best-selling series of pansies in North America. Their 8 cm wide blooms light up a container; they are the perfect design solution for edible pots full of green. The flowers have a mild wintergreen taste, and they're great in salads.

### Ⓑ Kale 'Pigeon Red'
*Brassica oleracea* var. *acephala;* flowering cabbage

Kale is easy to grow and adds both shape and texture to a container. Be warned that it is very aggressive and will push out any plant beside it as it expands. Kale is a vitamin- and antioxidant-packed superfood that you can eat raw, dry into chips or cook in soups and sautés. It thrives in cooler temperatures, which bring out richer colour and keep it from bolting; it is ideal for a fall rotation.

### Ⓒ Tomato 'Patio'
*Lycopersicon lycospersicum*

Its compact habit, ease of growth and prolific yield has made 'Patio' one of the best-selling tomatoes in North America. For years, it was one of the only reliable varieties that didn't have to be staked. Being determinate, it produces flushes of tomatoes that ripen about the same time, making it a feast or famine situation. It's convenient to grow but doesn't taste quite as good as many indeterminate types, so you need to decide which feature you want more.

### Ⓓ Fennel
*Foeniculum vulgare*

see p. 78

### Ⓔ Parsley 'Triple Curled'
*Petroselinum crispum*

see p. 171

# NATURALLY NASTURTIUMS

**Height:** to 80 cm • **Spread:** to 60 cm

NASTURTIUMS ADD SPRING to the step of any container they're in with their vivacious round, green leaves and vibrant flowers that seem to appear out of nowhere. Add their peppery taste to that and you have a winner that no edible garden should be without. With a surprising variety of seeds available, you can even pick your favourite colour.

**A** Nasturtium 'Whirlybird Mix'

**B** Bell pepper 'Green Bell'

**C** Chives

**D** Parsley 'Triple Curled'

**Recommended container size:** 30–40 cm across

The Salisbury production team put this container together, and I fell for it instantly. Its colours and airy buoyancy are so full of youthful enthusiasm. Everything here seems to be reaching out for something beyond the container's confines, and the plants are all so loosely growing that the leaves intertwine and emerge out of each other.

This is the colour green at its most exuberant. The variegation in the nasturtium leaves mimicks dappled sunlight as the various shapes of tall chives, dense parsley and overhanging pepper leaves contrast and complement each other.

Put this container in a sunny spot where the natural light will keep it

Nasturtiums grow like weeds and will be spilling out of any container you put them in by midsummer.

vibrant. Everything here can handle a lot of heat, but you will need to keep it well watered later in summer. The nasturtiums and parsley will mound ever higher up the pepper and chive stems. When the bell peppers form, they will add a glossy focal point so striking you might just leave them there.

You have all the elements here to take a summer salad of fresh greens from good to great. Sweet peppers, fresh chives and a touch of parsley, topped with peppery nasturtium flowers, will add a lot of personality to lettuce.

## Spotlight on Nasturtiums

Even though using it as an edible flower seems novel to us, the soft-spoken nasturtium has been cultivated as such for centuries in Europe. In 17th-century France it was even used to ward off starvation.

The easiest way to grow nasturtiums is also the cheapest. Like many veggies these flowers don't transplant well, so the best way to grow them is from seed. Soak the large seeds overnight for faster germination and simply poke them into moist soil.

The most likely obstacle to growing nasturtiums will be the high-quality soil in your container. Too many nutrients will make nasturtiums pour forth lots of leaves, but few flowers. Luckily, the leaves are gorgeous so this really isn't a problem.

Both the leaves and the flowers have the same peppery taste that I would compare to radish with a hint of lemon. While the flowers burst with colour, if you use intact leaves as well,

Nasturtiums come in a surprising array of colours, like these 'Butter Cream' ones from Renee's Garden.

you'll have crisp, circular elements in your dishes.

My favourite use for the flowers is nasturtium butter. Chop the flowers very fine and mix them into softened unsalted butter. The more flowers, the more peppery the butter. If you really want to spice it up, throw in a little garlic. Then chill the butter until you're ready to use it. It gives a delicious zing to anything you add it to and comes with a festive, confetti-like appearance.

---

### Ⓐ Nasturtium 'Whirlybird Mix'
*Tropaeolum majus;* Indian cress

Nasturtium is a South American native that grows quickly and easily, putting on a big show from spring till fall for the cost of a few seeds. 'Whirlybird' is an old-fashioned variety that I like because it's reliable and grows like a weed. If you're dealing with a specific colour scheme there's a host of new mono-coloured nasturtiums out there, from cream to dark red.

### Ⓑ Bell pepper 'Green Bell'
*Capsicum annuum*

see p. 159

### Ⓒ Chives
*Allium schoenoprasum*

Chives bring a lot to any container garden. They have a delicate onion flavour that is perfect in dishes where onions would be overpowering. Straight, vertical leaves bring a rare architectural presence to herb gardens, and in summer, light purple flowers will bring bees and other beneficial insects onto your patio. The younger growth tastes best, especially when fresh. They will self-seed widely if you let them.

### Ⓓ Parsley 'Triple Curled'
*Petroselinum crispum*

Historically, 'Triple Curled' parsley has been famous as a garnish while its more flavourful Italian cousin has taken the culinary glory. Its fresh, crisp taste makes it excellent in many dishes, however. Add it to meat dishes, vegetable dishes or tabbouleh. It freshens the breath after eating garlic and onions. It's not very drought tolerant, and the new growth is most flavourful. Pinch it regularly and it will get bushy, dense and gorgeous.

**Height:** to 1.3 m • **Spread:** to 90 cm  /

**MOSQUITOES ARE A FACT** of life in Canada, but dousing our skin in DEET doesn't have to be. This container, though non-edible, is perfect to grow on your patio, in your gazebo or anywhere you like to sit and unwind in the evenings. You could also break it up into smaller pots to create a scented perimeter.

Ⓐ Citronella geranium

Ⓑ Marigold 'Lemon Gem'

Ⓒ Lemon grass

Ⓓ Catnip

Ⓔ Ageratum 'Artist Purple'

Ⓕ Lemon thyme

**Recommended container size:**
70 cm across

People tend to think that the only plant that naturally repels mosquitoes is citronella geranium and are surprised to learn how many plants there are. It's true that many of the others have neither the "street-cred" nor the marketing that citronella has, but they are effective nonetheless.

When designing a pot for such a specific task as mosquito control, try to make it attractive enough that it will blend in with the rest of your containers. If it looks utilitarian you'll tend to think of it as a tool and won't display it with the pretty things.

Catnip contains a naturally occurring insect repellent (nepetalactone), which is effective at keeping most creepy-crawly and flying pests out of the vicinity. Spread fresh catnip

Tagetes marigolds offer excellent pest protection; plus they are prettier and taste much better than chemicals.

leaves in an ant-infested area for a useful, though temporary, way of telling them they aren't welcome.

Ask for signet marigolds for repelling mosquitoes. They're an old-fashioned variety so they won't be as easy to find as the French types (which are excellent for other pest control), but many garden centres are starting to carry them again in response to demand.

Make sure not to toss your citronella plant out at seasons' end. Geraniums are easy to overwinter and, in spring, you can take cuttings and build a mosquito-repelling army of citronella plants that you can use in all the containers around your sitting area.

## Using Citronella

There's a debate about how effective citronella geraniums really are in deterring "skeeters." It's a fact that the insects hate the smell and will avoid it; the tricky part is making sure they smell it. If the plant is too far away from you or if the wind is blowing the scent away, the bugs will bite.

Geraniums also don't have nearly the concentration of citronella as the essential oils or candles do. The reality of using plants is that you never get the concentration of chemicals that you will with products manufactured for that purpose.

Still, you don't need to keep a citronella plant in your lap to make sure it works. The scent is released when the leaves are crushed. Simply grab a few leaves, crush them in your hands and rub them generously on any exposed skin including, unless you don't like the smell, your neck and face. Make sure not to take too many leaves when you do this; the plant needs them too.

This planter from Wellington Gardens in Edmonton blends lemon thyme with non-edibles for a dramatic effect.

### A Citronella geranium

*Pelargonium citrosum*

Although citonella oil is harvested from another plant, citronella geranium contains the same essential oils, looks great in containers and is easy to grow. It sports intriguingly shaped leaves and lavender flowers, but its real value is in its mosquito repelling qualities. You can easily root cuttings by putting the tips in water and planting them when they have adequate roots. Look for starter plants early because they always sell out.

### B Marigold 'Lemon Gem'

*Tagetes tenuifolia;* signet marigold

These are classic marigolds that combine the pest-controlling benefits of French marigolds with a statuesque habit and lacy leaves punctuated by scores of single, yellow sundrop flowers, which are edible. It will grow easily in full sun into a bushy filler plant, contributing finely cut leaves to the overall architecture. You'll notice a lemony fragrance surrounding it; it's a natural mosquito deterrent.

### C Lemon grass

*Cymbopogon citratus*

see p. 71

### D Catnip

*Nepeta cataria*

see p. 191

### E Ageratum 'Artist Purple'

*Ageratum houstonianum;* floss flower

Ageratum is a classic bedding plant, perhaps out of place in this book. Dozens of hybrids have been developed, the latest being the Artist Series by Proven Winners. It provides mounds of colour all summer and has better heat tolerance than its predecessors. It's not edible but it does deter mosquitoes by emitting the chemical coumarin, which the flying pests hate. Ageratum is an excellent addition for a splash of colour.

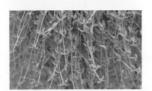

### F Lemon thyme

*Thymus* x *citriodorus*

see p. 187

# BRAIN BOOSTER

**Height:** to 70 cm • **Spread:** to 70 cm

**THIS RECIPE CONTAINS POTENT** herbs that people across Asia have been using to increase mental function for centuries. It's perfect for people who are interested in a doctor-supervised program of fresh herbal supplements. The herbs are rare in Canada but are available from Richters.

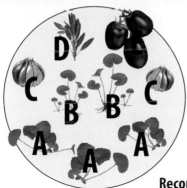

**A** Brahmi

**B** Gotu kola

**C** Garlic

**D** Sage

**E** Tomato 'Health Kick'

**Recommended container size:** 60–70 cm across

While 'Health Kick' tomato is one of the first edibles that have been bred specifically for enhanced health benefits, there will be many more in the years ahead. This tomato makes an aesthetically average centrepiece for a container full of fairly shapeless ingredients; this container isn't grown for its looks.

Beyond something to keep the weight of its tomatoes from dragging it down, 'Health Kick' shouldn't need a large support. It's tasty and determinate, so you can enjoy a trickle of ripening tomatoes throughout late summer and into fall.

If brahmi's genus name *Bacopa* sounds familiar, it is. Bacopa is the brand-name of an intensely popular annual basket stuffer from Proven Winners. Although it's called bacopa, its genus is *Sutera*, and it's neither closely related to brahmi nor is it edible as far as I know.

The garlic may be a herb too far for some people because the overwintering required can be a hassle; it may be easier to just buy it fresh from the farmers' market. Garlic prevents blood clots by thinning the blood and has been found to help prevent damage to cells caused by stress. It tastes pretty good too.

Brahmi will offer small white flowers that are similar to the ubiquitous bedding plant bacopa, although the plants are very different.

It surprises people to hear how many health benefits are in soft-spoken garden sage. It's a known memory enhancer and may help guard against Alzheimer's disease.

## A Word of Caution

Health conscious Canadians are taking to natural remedies in a big way. I don't want to discourage that, but, based on some troubling things I've heard, I do want to put a warning out there to anyone interested in taking medicinal herbs.

The majority of active ingredients in the pills prescribed today are derived from plants. The all-natural chemicals found in leaves and roots across the world have led to incredible scientific breakthroughs. When we take herbs directly, we're going back to the source of those breakthroughs.

When you grow medicinal herbs, you're basically growing pills. It's very important to give herbs the same respect you do pills. Like any drug, herbs are beneficial in moderation and potentially dangerous in excess.

Herbs also take a long time to work. A supplement such as brahmi takes years for noticeable results. It's tempting to think, "If I take more, it will work faster," but it's vital to stay within the recommended dosage.

While I want to inspire people to grow the plants they use, either as food or otherwise, I don't endorse

Quinoa is skyrocketing to popularity as a filling, healthy grain that is one of the better complex carbohydrates out there.

Use caution when ingesting medicinal herbs, and be aware that some plants appearing on some herb lists are highly toxic if used incorrectly.

taking any medicinal herb without knowing its full effects. Before starting a medicinal herb program, take the time to consult your doctor. If you are pregnant, planning to become pregnant or breastfeeding, take extra precautions.

### Ⓐ Brahmi
*Bacopa monnieri;* water hyssop

Brahmi has been used in India for thousands of years. It contains bacosides, which help the neurons in our brains transmit information, and in doing so increases memory retention, concentration and even IQ. It's also a powerful antioxidant and helps prevent neurodegenerative diseases by protecting us from free radicals. Research is ongoing, but so far Western science is confirming ancient Eastern thought.

### Ⓑ Gotu kola
*Centella asiatica*

Native to tropical Asia, this humble herb has been used in traditional medicines for centuries but is only rarely grown in Canada. It's an easy-to-grow, creeping plant that tolerates poor soils and wet, boggy conditions. Sri Lankan cooks often use it as a salad green, but it's best known as one of the best herbs in the world for everything from treating open sores to relieving tension and as a cerebral tonic.

### Ⓒ Garlic
*Allium sativum*

see p. 54

### Ⓓ Sage
*Salvia officinalis*

see p. 62

### Ⓔ Tomato 'Health Kick'
*Lycopersicon lycopersicum*

This determinate plum tomato is easy to grow in pots and contains about 50 percent more lycopene than most varieties. Lycopene is a powerful antioxidant that has been found, among other things, to help fight certain cancers including prostate, and we get almost all of our lycopene intact from tomatoes. 'Health Kick' came from conventional breeding and isn't genetically modified.

**Height:** to 1 m • **Spread:** to 70 cm

**THESE CONTAINERS ARE** a grab-bag of medicinal treats, and the various plants have been known to treat most any minor malady that afflicts you. There could easily be other plants here, such as aloe, and you can customize your container-bound medicine cabinet to your needs.

 **A** Lovage

**B** Catnip

**C** Peppermint

**D** Sage

**E** Echinacea 'Magnus'

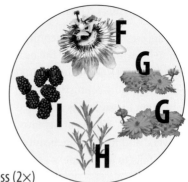

**F** Passionflower

**G** Calendula 'Bon Bon Mix'

**H** Winter savory

**I** Blackberry 'Prime-Ark 45'

**Recommended container size:** 60 cm across (2×)

---

Lovage was cultivated 2000 years ago as an aphrodisiac. Today, the leaves are commonly dried and steeped into tea to aid digestion and soothe sore throats.

I included blackberries because, besides wanting to make the point that fruit is a healer in and of itself, they contain the potent deflammatory agent and antioxidant anthocyanin. This cancer-fighting chemical is also what gives blackberries their colour.

Catnip has been used to treat cold and flu symptoms for centuries. It induces sweating without raising body temperature and acts as a sedative.

The most medicinally effective part of echinacea is the root, which you harvest after the plant has died back from frost. If the plant is less than three to four years old, taking even a part of the root can kill it. Luckily, echinacea grows easily from seed. Cut off the large, mature heads, put them in a paper bag and hang them upside down to dry. Once the seeds are fully dried, refrigerate them in a sealed jar for spring sowing.

In most cases throughout this book I'm deliberately avoiding providing recommended dosages for herbal medicines. I feel that these details are best worked out with your family doctor, pharmacist or herbalist. I've also deliberately excluded the many herbicidal herbs, such as St. John's wort, which are toxic if the dosage is exceeded. I want to stress that medicinal herbs are just like pills and must be approached with caution and respect.

## Passionflower 101

The species in question acquired the name *incarnata* because the beautiful complexity of the flower reminded 16th-century Spanish Christian missionaries of the passion of the Christ. It's one of my favourite flowers, and its intricate beauty never fails to dazzle me.

*Passiflora edulis* flowers are one of the most complex and stunning blooms in the plant world, and they develop into delcicious tropical fruit.

Passionflower is well known for its ability to calm the nerves and soothe anxiety. A teaspoon of dried passionflower in tea has been known to act as a relaxing sedative. In a stress-addled society, this reputation has made it very popular with businesses looking to sell essential oils.

Passionflowers are more commonly sold as ornamental plants than as herbs. Check the tag before buying because, although the species look very similar, chemically speaking they differ widely. *Passiflora caerulea*, which is the one you'll probably find first, contains trace amounts of cyanide and shouldn't be taken internally. If in doubt, go online and order the real thing from a specialized company such as Richters.

If you're interested in growing passion fruit, look for *Passiflora edulis*. While getting edible passion fruits to ripen in Canada is possible, it requires years of patiently nurturing the plant to a sufficient size and then a freakishly long, hot summer for the fruit to ripen. You'd have to really, really love passion fruit to do it.

 **Lovage**
*Levisticum officinale*

Lovage is a big, versatile herb that can grow to 2 m tall and can be used for everything from salads to antiseptic. It's easy to grow and, if you overwinter it, will become too large for all but the largest of containers. I prefer to keep mine cut back so that I can enjoy the leaves, which have a complex celery-like taste in salads, without the plant dominating the design.

### B Catnip
*Nepeta cataria*

see p. 191

### C Peppermint
*Mentha x piperita*

see p. 62

### D Sage
*Salvia officinalis*

see p. 62

### E Echinacea 'Magnus'
*Echinacea purpurea;* purple coneflower

Echinacea is one of the most popular supplements for strengthening the immune system. It is both easy to grow and gorgeous in the garden. It readily attracts bees and butterflies, and the rusty orange flower centres bring a colour rarely seen in the garden. Overwinter it in the garden and you'll have an impressive specimen in a few years.

### F Passionflower
*Passiflora incarnata;* maypop

This vine is easy to grow as long as you give it support. In summer it treats you with remarkable flowers that you'll recognize from essential oils packaging. If you're anywhere but Zone 2 or 3, I suggest keeping it safely confined to a container. It's a nasty weed in the U.S. and, beautiful as it is, you don't want it taking over your yard.

### G Calendula 'Bon Bon Mix'
*Calendula officinalis*

see p. 110

### H Winter savory
*Satureja montana*

see p. 63

### I Blackberry 'Prime-Ark 45'
*Rubus fruticosus*

see p. 111

# GRILL MAGIC

**Height:** to 1 m • **Spread:** to 60 cm

**IF YOU LOVE GRILLING,** this recipe is custom made for you. Purist grillers know the difference between the flavour of dried herbs and fresh herbs on their meat and potatoes. This recipe allows you access to fresh herbs whenever you grill, and if there's something you want that isn't here, you can just substitute it in.

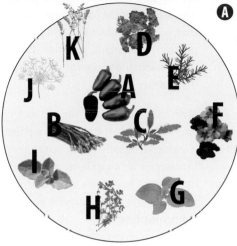

A  Jalapeno pepper 'Mucho Nacho'

B  Garlic chives

C  Sage 'Tricolor'

D  Parsley 'Triple Curled'

E  Rosemary 'Barbeque'

F  Nasturtium 'Alaska Mix'

G  Mint 'Italian Spice'

H  Lemon thyme

I  Greek oregano

J  Dill 'Bouquet'

K  Bronze fennel

**Recommended container size:**
45–60 cm across

---

This container is the spice rack to your outdoor kitchen, and you'll want to keep it within quick pinching distance of the barbecue. It's designed so a sprig of rosemary, a clump of dill leaves or a ripe jalapeno are always at your disposal. Harvesttime is whenever you're cooking something juicy that needs an extra twist of flavour.

When using herbs for cooking, there are a few rules to remember. New growth is always the freshest, so nip off the top bits, but never more than a third of the stem. Pinch off flowers as soon as you see them forming, or they will affect the taste. The most flavourful time to harvest is in the morning, but as we don't normally barbecue in the morning, it's better they are picked fresh in the evening.

I used a terracotta pot for this one. Most of the plants here are heat-loving herbs that love to have their roots warmed. If it's too much watering for you, plastic will keep the roots moist longer.

Don't plant dill near fennel if you want to harvest the seeds of either,

Every time you harvest a herb it grows in fuller, until your purple sage looks like this one, which is two years old.

as the cross-pollination will prevent seed formation. I prefer the leaves of both plants to the seeds.

Besides being gorgeous and great in salads, nasturtiums are useful as bait to lure nasty pests away from your prized vegetables. Direct seed one or two nasturtiums in your containers, and aphids and slugs will be irresistibly drawn to them. Once the pests have taken up residence on the nasturtiums (leaving the other plants alone), snip off the flowers and replace them with fresh seed. They grow so quickly and easily you won't notice they're gone.

## Making Rosemary Skewers

If you like shish kebabs then you'll love this. Once your rosemary plant has 25–30 cm long woody stems, cut a handful off at the base. Keep in mind that, as this involves taking a good portion of the plant, you may want to plant extra if you want some left over for seasoning.

Strip the stems except the top inch or two and whittle the base into a point if it's exceptionally blunt. Soak them in water for about an hour as you chop up cubes of beef, pork, mushrooms, tomatoes and fresh jalapeno peppers from your container.

Spear and cook the kebabs on medium heat, and the flavour of the rosemary stem will infuse into the food. For more flavour, chop a quick sachet of oregano, sage and chives to sprinkle over top.

---

### Ⓐ Jalapeno pepper 'Mucho Nacho'
*Capsicum annuum*

A fairly new variety of jalapeno, 'Mucho Nacho' boasts large, 10 cm long peppers with thick walls. They are early, prolific and more tolerant of chilly June nights than most peppers, which makes them ideal for Canadian patios. Their heat will vary dramatically (from 5000 to 30,000 Scoville units) from plant to plant, and even on the same plant. Use them fresh or dry them for spices.

### Ⓑ Garlic chives
*Allium tuberosum*

see p. 55

### Ⓒ Sage 'Tricolor'
*Salvia officinalis*

see p. 62

### ⑪ Parsley 'Triple Curled'
*Petroselinum crispum*

see p. 171

### ⑫ Rosemary 'Barbeque'
*Rosmarinus officinalis*

Although it's a relatively recent arrival on the herb scene, this one is becoming a "must-have" for any serious griller. The taste is tangier and spicier than other varieties, and its tall, upright stems are perfect for garnish stalks for steaks and as shish kebab spears (don't forget to soak them in water for an hour first). Grow it just like other varieties.

### ⑬ Nasturtium 'Alaska Mix'
*Tropaeolum majus*

see p. 217

### ⑭ Mint 'Italian Spice'
*Mentha* hybrids

see p. 95

### ⑮ Lemon thyme
*Thymus* x *citriodorus;* creeping thyme

Lemon thyme is a delightfully miniature plant that doesn't grow large but packs a big culinary and ornamental punch. The subtle flavour doesn't have any of the bitterness of regular thyme and is perfect for flavouring desserts or teas. It's invasive, so it needs to be kept container-bound, but on the other hand it's easy to propagate by cuttings.

### ⑯ Greek oregano
*Origanum vulgare* var. *hirtum*

see p. 102

### ⑰ Dill 'Bouquet'
*Anethum graveolens*

see p. 103

### ⑱ Bronze fennel
*Foeniculum vulgare* 'Purpureum'

see p. 78

# CAT POTS

**Height:** to 1 m • **Spread:** to 70 cm

**I'M A SELF-CONFESSED CAT LOVER,** and as such I couldn't miss the opportunity to let my furry rascals get in on the edible fun. This container is dedicated to scheming felines everywhere. Put it outside and they will chew, rub and roll in it, and though, being cats, they will show no appreciation, it'll still be a great show.

**Ⓐ** Catnip

**Ⓑ** Lemon grass

**Ⓒ** Valerian

**Ⓓ** Cat grass

**Recommended container size:**
45–60 cm across

As plant lovers know, cats will chew, and shred, almost anything they can get their pink paws around. Ideally, this container will keep cats away from the plants you don't want destroyed. As anyone with a pristine scratching post and a torn-up couch can tell you, it doesn't always work that way. You will, however, have a blast watching your cats engage with the plants, just as my wife and I did.

The scent of lemon grass attracts cats, and they eat it as they would any grass or your favourite plant. If you want to use it as a culinary herb, consider growing two and keeping one out of feline reach.

The active ingredient in valerian, valerinone, is very similar to the active ingredient in catnip. It's a stimulant in cats, though it's a sedative in humans. Some is found in the leaves but the majority is in the roots, so your cat may not find your valerian appealing until you chop, dry and

A healthy supply of catnip will keep your cats blissfully happy and very entertaining for as long as it's growing.

stuff the root into homemade toys. You can buy valerian essential oils, but they are for human use and are too concentrated for kitties.

Catnip drives most cats crazy (some are immune to it), but to different degrees. I've seen it sedate, excite or make them just plain mean. Although they eat it, it's the smell that gets them high. They rub against the leaves to crush them and release the scent. Eating the leaves is just another way to get closer to the scent, and ironically it is what puts the cats to sleep.

Catnip's active ingredient, nepetalactone, is a hallucinogenic and possibly an aphrodisiac, especially in female cats. Nepetalactone is also very effective at repelling mosquitoes.

## Cats and Grass

There are multiple theories about why cats eat grass. Some people say it's to help them pass furballs by vomiting, and others claim it's an instinctual need for niacin and fibre. All we know for sure is that cats, from tabbys to tigers, do it compulsively and show no sign of stopping.

Cat grass, which is essentially oat sprouts, is meant to provide indoor cats with an easily digestible alternative to the grass they crave. There's no evidence that cats need grass, but they do seem to love it, so there's really no harm in letting them have it.

Buy cat grass in seed packets and sprinkle the seed over moist soil. It

Chives attract much-needed bees into the yard, so always let a few of them go to bloom. Although toxic to cats, they play an important role in increasing the biodiversity in the yard.

will sprout in a few days and, as your cat mows it down, should keep growing. Don't confuse cat grass, which is for cats, with wheat grass (*Triticum aestivum*), which is what you see at health-conscious juice bars and is for humans.

Cat grass should keep your cats from eating other plants in the house, and it's easy to grow.

### Ⓐ Catnip
*Nepeta cataria*

For centuries, catnip has been used as a medicinal cure for a variety of ailments. Today, we associate it more with strung out cats and countless catnip-stuffed toys lining pet store shelves. It's easy to grow (if you can keep the cats off it), but keep an eye on it to make sure it doesn't crowd out its neighbours. Once the stems are 20 cm long, hang bunches of it upside down until dry.

### Ⓑ Lemon grass
*Cymbopogon citratus*

p. 71

### Ⓒ Valerian
*Valeriana officinalis;* garden heliotrope

Valerian grows to 1.5 m tall and boasts sweet-smelling flowers in summer. It's beautiful in the garden or inside as long-lasting cut flowers. The ancient Greeks used it as a cure for insomnia. Today, people use the stringy roots in sedative teas or to make toys that cats find irresistible. It's been called "poor man's valium" because it has many of the same effects. Talk to a doctor before using it.

### Ⓓ Cat grass
*Avena sativa;* common oats

Cats have a natural craving for grass that, if they don't have access to it, often leads them to eat houseplants instead. Cat grass is among the easiest plants to grow; simply sprinkle seed onto moist soil and wait a few days. It's actually a common cereal, though you'll find it in specially branded packages with smiling kitties on the front. Sprinkle fresh seed every week to keep your crop lush and healthy.

# BOTTOMS UP

**Height:** to 1 m • **Spread:** to 70 cm

**THIS DESIGN WOULD BE** a conversation starter on the patio of any outdoor bar. Although you're probably not going to be making fresh beer, there are a variety of drink fixings including fresh lemons for your summer beer, celery for your Caesars and mint for your mohitos. If you're ambitious, you can even make your own wine.

Admittedly, I got carried away with this one. I wanted to make pots that sat on a patio bar to impress everyone who approached them. If the hops and grapes are too much commitment, you could easily pare it down.

A Grape 'Riesling'

B Grape 'Pinot Noir'

C Celery 'Utah 52–70'

D Mint 'Margarita'

E Strawberry 'Tristar'

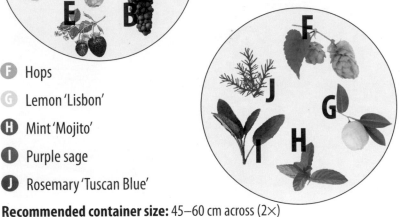

F Hops

G Lemon 'Lisbon'

H Mint 'Mojito'

I Purple sage

J Rosemary 'Tuscan Blue'

**Recommended container size:** 45–60 cm across (2×)

---

Hops will grow like crazy and climb anything they can get leverage from, like these at the McGill University campus in Montreal.

The great thing here is that, since you probably won't serve enough drinks to use everything, you'll be able to be generous with the mint and rosemary. Make sure to keep the mint pruned so that it doesn't gobble up its neighbours. I included strawberries because I love to throw a few into my Pimms cocktail.

It was a touch choice between lemons and limes, as both are common in drinks. Whichever you use, make sure to bring it indoors to enjoy as a houseplant during winter.

Mohitos have enjoyed a surge of popularity in recent years, and bars and cocktail lounges everywhere are cashing in on this trendy drink. Instead of paying lounge prices, you can make your own. Use fresh lime (preferably grown yourself), some 'Mohito' mint leaves, cane sugar (I don't recommend growing your own sugar cane) and white rum and top it off with sparkling water. If you want to be traditionally Cuban, use spearmint leaves.

## Growing Grapes in Pots

Yes, you can grow grapevines in pots. That's the good news; the bad news is that it's a little more involved than growing other fruit. If you're a grape lover and/or wine maker, however, you shouldn't let the lack of a yard stop you.

The first challenge is that grapevines are bigger than most fruits. They need thick, extensive vines in order to yield, and those vines must be supported by a large root system. To accommodate the roots, and to make it easier to overwinter, you'll need at least a 75 litre container (a little smaller than a half whisky barrel).

Your grape will need to spend its first few years growing and thickening its vines. Nip off any flowers that appear so it keeps its focus, and make an effort to train the vines along the support. Grapes like to throw out more flowers than they can support, so you're doing it a favour. The larger support you have, the bigger vines and higher yield you'll have.

Heartbreaking as it will be, snip any grapes off that appear the first year (below left) so the plant puts more energy into making vines (below right).

Your pruning goal in the first two years will be to establish a main trunk with about four strong vines coming off of it. When winter comes, prune these back so there are just a few buds on each.

I discuss winterizing on pages 27–29, and grapes are no different. If you're on a high apartment balcony, make sure to insulate well against the wind. If you're going to be moving your container around, I suggest wheels on the bottom—that pot gets heavy.

### Ⓐ Grape 'Riesling'

*Vitis vinifera*

This is a classic grape of German and, increasingly, French white wines. Very aromatic and high in acidity, its flavour has a reputation for changing based on where it's grown. It makes stellar ice wine and table wine in the Niagara and Okanagan regions, but in cooler regions it probably won't ripen before the first frosts. Choose a variety with a hardiness level that you're willing to work with to overwinter; the more classic the grape, the less hardy it tends to be.

### Ⓑ Grape 'Pinot Noir'

*Vitis vinifera*

One of the oldest cultivated grape varieties in existence, 'Pinot Noir' is a cool-weather grape, which makes it suitable for warmer Canadian regions (or even cooler ones if you give it special treatment). This is a grape for the experienced grower/wine-maker, for though it's known for making some of the best wines in the world, it can be difficult to work with. Take care in overwintering.

### Ⓒ Celery 'Utah 52-70'

*Apium graveolens*

see p. 137

### Ⓓ Mint 'Margarita'

*Mentha* hybrids

This introduction by mint breeder Jim Westerfield is attractive in containers and versatile at the bar. It sports large, burgundy-rimmed leaves with deep grooves. With its fruity lime smell and taste you can use it in iced teas, margaritas (of course) and pretty much any other mixed drink. Although not quite as aggressive as other mints, I still recommend keeping it contained. It has a tall, upright habit and grows in almost any soil.

### ⓔ Strawberry 'Tristar'
*Fragaria* hybrids

see p. 208

### ⓕ Hops
*Humulus lupulus*

The term "hops" actually refers to the female flower clusters on *Humulus lupulus*, which are the recognizably bitter flavouring and stabilizing agent in beer. Dedicated home-brewers do use them for beer, though you'll need a lot of trellis space in order to get the necessary number of flower clusters. You'll need to overwinter your hop plant to get a decent yield, but its hardiness makes this fairly routine.

### ⓖ Lemon 'Lisbon'
*Citrus limon*

Lemons are ideal for container growing. They need very little pruning, will grow for years in a 20 L pot without needing transplanting, and bring tropical colour and texture to the patio. 'Lisbon' lemons are similar to 'Eureka,' the common supermarket type, only a bit more sour. A higher concentration of citric acid makes them ideal for lemonade or adding zest to summer cocktails. 'Lisbon' sports a lot of thorns, so be cautious with it.

### ⓗ Mint 'Mojito'
*Mentha* hybrids

The rooftop herb garden at Toronto's Fairmont Royal York has an entire raised bed of this stuff because mojitos are that popular. If you love the drink, grow the herb. It has a milder flavour than other mints. Like all mints, keep it container bound or your whole yard will turn into a mojito bar (unless that's the intention). Use the freshest young leaves for the best flavour.

### ⓘ Purple sage
*Salvia officinalis* 'Purpurascens'

see p. 163

### ⓙ Rosemary 'Tuscan Blue'
*Rosmarinus officinalis*

see p. 217

# SWEET SURRENDER

**Height:** to 1 m • **Spread:** to 70 cm

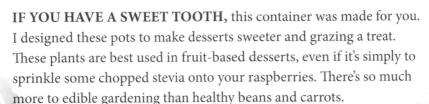

**IF YOU HAVE A SWEET TOOTH,** this container was made for you. I designed these pots to make desserts sweeter and grazing a treat. These plants are best used in fruit-based desserts, even if it's simply to sprinkle some chopped stevia onto your raspberries. There's so much more to edible gardening than healthy beans and carrots.

**Ⓐ** Calamondin orange

**Ⓑ** Pansy 'Frizzle Sizzle Mix'

**Ⓒ** Strawberry 'Berries Galore'

**Ⓓ** Borage

**Ⓔ** Stevia

**Ⓕ** Pineapple sage

**Ⓖ** Sweet cicely

**Ⓗ** Rose geranium

**Ⓘ** Lemon balm

**Ⓙ** Mint 'Chocolate'

**Recommended container size:** 45 cm by 45 cm (2×)

---

These ingredients were made to add extra touches to fruity desserts. Some of them are straight forward, like using stevia or sweet cicely instead of refined sugar, and some, like candying borage and pansy flowers (see p. 166), are more complicated.

I found two wooden crates that seemed made for this recipe. When you're making a whimsical design, look around for whimsical containers. Second-hand they usually aren't expensive; just make sure to either avoid treated wood or line it with plastic. I would avoid old pots with painted interiors altogether, as there may be lead involved.

The geranium brings a twist of colour in its leaf, and you can use it in unique edible creations. The perfume-scented leaves enhance the flavour of fruits such as raspberries, apricots and peaches. You can also use it in pound cakes and citrus sorbets or to brew a soothing tea.

The strawberries go well with anything, if any of them actually make it into the house without being eaten. I included the calamondin because it provides a generous amount of fruit and is the easiest orange to grow in our climate. It makes an excellent marmalade even if it's a little bitter to be a grazing citrus.

## Growing Citrus

It's easy to grow citrus in Canada as long as you're realistic with the varieties you choose. Stick to acidic types, like lemons, limes, kumquats and calamondins. They're smaller, need less light and yield much faster than the sweet Florida crops we see in the supermarkets.

Calamondins are the most popular citrus in Canada because they are the easiest to grow and yield more

Calamondin oranges are the easiest citrus to grow and they thrive in containers, inside in winter and outside in summer.

than most. As the most ornamental variety, they also make a beautiful houseguest in winter.

Although not true oranges, calamondins produce scores of 4 cm fruit that are preceded by intoxicating yet delicate, white flowers. You will need to be the bee and pollinate your calamondin. Simply rub a small, dry paintbrush or Q-tip in all the flowers to spread the pollen around.

The fruit is edible (peels and all), and although it's sour, it's perfect for making marmalades or adding to summer drinks. It makes a zesty lemon substitute. Don't be in a rush to pick the oranges. They are gorgeous ripening on the branch and last for months, sweetening gradually as they hang.

Make sure to give it plenty of fertilizer and don't let it dry to the point of stress. When you take it outside in spring, wait until the nights have lost their chill and acclimatize it with initial protection from the afternoon sun.

### Ⓐ Calamondin orange
*Citrofortunella microcarpa*

Calamondins are the easiest oranges to grow in containers. Lush, dark green–leafed plants yield fistfuls of fruit throughout summer. You may be excited when they turn orange, but resist picking them until they are almost falling off the stem. The trees will last for years, seldom needing transplanting or pruning and not getting overly large.

### Ⓑ Pansy 'Frizzle Sizzle Mix'
*Viola* x *wittrockiana*

see p. 167

### **C** Strawberry 'Berries Galore'
*Fragaria* hybrids

see p. 213

### **D** Borage
*Borago officinalis*

see p. 110

### **E** Stevia
*Stevia rebaudiana*

see p. 133

### **F** Pineapple sage
*Salvia elegans*

see p. 213

### **G** Sweet cicely
*Myrrhis odorata*

This Central European native brings finely cut leaves and culinary versatility to the garden. It grows up to 2 m tall if you overwinter it and will crowd out its neighbours if you let it. Its leaves are widely used in German and Scandinavian cooking for their anise taste. Lately it has come into fashion as a sugar substitute. It's closely related to chervil.

### **H** Rose geranium
*Pelargonium graveolens*

see p. 229

### **I** Lemon balm
*Melissa officinalis*

see p. 123

### **J** Mint 'Chocolate'
*Mentha x piperita*

The first time you taste this leaf you'll do a double take; it really does taste like chocolate. Closely related to peppermint, 'Chocolate' mint was bred to add flavour to brownies or any other sweet treat. Its green leaves grow atop attractive brown stems. Like all the mints, you'll want to keep it in containers in warmer regions.

# CINDER BLOCK PLANTER

**Height:** to 1 m • **Spread:** to 2 m

**AS EDIBLE GARDENING IN** raised beds becomes more popular, so too does the concern about the chemicals that treated lumber can leech into plants' roots and, from there, into the foliage and fruit. Cinder blocks are easy to assemble, environmentally friendly, versatile and safe for edibles. Consider them when you're building your next raised bed, as long as you're not fussy about the slightly industrial look that comes with them.

- **A** Tomato 'Lemon Boy'
- **B** Beans 'Tricolor Bush'
- **C** Lemon grass
- **D** Oregano 'Hot & Spicy'
- **E** Wormwood
- **F** Strawberry 'Tristar'
- **G** Nasturtium 'Alaska Mix'
- **H** Curry plant
- **I** Tomato 'Tiny Tim'
- **J** Chives
- **K** Rosemary 'Tuscan Blue'
- **L** Sage
- **M** Basil
- **N** English thyme

**Recommended container size:** 2 m across or as desired

Cinder blocks provide an alternative for those people who want a raised planter but are sceptical about using treated wood. The blocks last forever and provide small, ongoing doses of calcium for the plants. It's great to recycle, but make sure the blocks you use didn't have a past life at a chemical plant or other place where they could have absorbed unsavoury chemicals.

While the width of the blocks (usually they're about 20 cm by 40 cm) discourages some people, try to see it as an opportunity over an obstacle. The built-in holes in the blocks can be planted with herbs or edible flowers, leaving the middle open for you to plant large and potentially aggressive vegetables without fear of competition. If one hole is too small for what you want to plant, use a hammer and chisel to eliminate the wall between the openings.

When planting in concrete, keep in mind that lime will leech into the soil and the root systems. While lime is a natural, welcome supplement to most veggies, especially peas, beans and cabbages, acid-loving edibles such as blueberries and radishes will resent that it makes the soil more alkaline. If you're concerned about the pH being too high, use a peat moss based medium to balance it out.

The concrete acts like a terracotta pot, absorbing moisture and heating up in the sun. Use heat-loving plants and avoid those that need a steady supply of moisture, such as tomatoes, cucumbers or strawberries, unless you're committed to watering daily. This is especially true in dry climates. Once the plants get larger, and through midsummer heat waves, you may want to invest in a drip irrigation system to keep them moist.

Growing in a cinder block planter is an easy way to build the shape of planter that best fits your yard.

I did the bulk of my planting in the small holes and reserved the centre for a tomato and bush beans, which are otherwise bad candidates for containers as they don't share well. Out of all the containers in my workshop, this one provided the most flavourful basil, thyme and sage. Plus the tomatoes didn't have a hint of blossom end-rot, adding evidence that the disease is caused as much by calcium deficiency as inconsistent watering.

## Be Creative

Cinder blocks are basically building blocks, so be creative when assembling your planter. Unlike wood, you don't have to worry about nails or whether or not you'll keep it there forever. While it will be sturdy enough to be permanent, you can also move it at will to another spot or configuration. A quick internet search will uncover a host of different designs, from simple one-tiered squares to elaborate

Although not the cooking curry, the silver-leafed curry plant adds striking colour and texture to containers.

vertical planters with built-in shelves and niches. You can make curved planters that wrap around sidewalks, rows of small squares for a formal herb garden, or even a compost pile.

Try a planter in one spot and, if you don't like it, move it to another spot in fall. If grey, industrial concrete isn't your thing, get the kids involved and paint the blocks in vivacious colours.

I tiered my planter, from one block high in the front to four high in the back, to make it more decorative. If you're growing large plants or root veggies, make it two blocks high at least. Just don't make the planter so wide that you can't comfortably reach the centre; I would max it out at 1.2 m wide.

If you're stacking the blocks for vertical gardening, experiment with trailing edibles such as strawberries (which will need to be in peat moss) and nasturtiums. Make sure the blocks are secured safely no matter how you stack them; their weight can make them a hazard for children.

Don't be afraid to add some garden ornaments to your planters. The Salisbury staff added these plastic bones for me.

Edamame beans are very popular in Asain cooking. These edible soybeans are surprisingly easy to grow.

Pole beans, like this 'Rattlesnake' mix from Renee's Garden, are easy to grow as long as you provide a support or trellis.

## Tips for Better Beans

Pound for pound, beans pack a bigger health benefit than almost anything else. They are full of protein, fibre and calcium. The United States Department of Agriculture ranks them as the best antioxidant food.

Make sure to grab some inoculant when you buy your seeds. Inoculant is actually microbacteria that cling to legume roots and allow them to fix usable nitrogen right out of thin air. It's yct another example of how plants are simply amazing.

Using inoculants means that you can fertilize your legumes less than other crops. It also means that they leave nitrogen in the soil for the next vegetable rotation to enjoy. Plant nitrogen lovers such as cauliflower and cabbage in the spot where the beans and peas were the previous year.

Like most veggies that are borne from flowers, bean plants will slow or stop producing new blooms if they think their job is done. Over-ripe beans on the vine will lead to no new flowers and no new beans. To avoid this, cut (never yank) your beans off the vine before the shells get tough. Leave an inch of stem on the bean and the nutrients will continue to feed it.

---

### Ⓐ **Tomato 'Lemon Boy'**
*Lycopersicon lycopersicum*

One of the most popular yellow tomatoes for home gardeners, 'Lemon Boy' is early (about 75 days), high yielding and easy to care for. It's indeterminate (and grows like a weed), so it will need staking. The tomatoes are sweet for their size and add a colourful twist to salsa or salads. It's resistant to most major tomato diseases, including fusarium wilt.

### Ⓑ Beans 'Tricolor Bush'

*Phaseolus vulgaris;* bush beans

It's not easy to make beans cool, but Renee's Garden managed it with their 'Tricolor Bush' mix. It's a blend of 'Golden Roc d'Or,' 'Purple Queen' and 'Green Slenderette' bush beans. As with all beans, just throw the seeds in moist soil and walk away. Keep dead leaves cleaned up to cut back on slugs, especially if the space is enclosed (as with this garden).

### Ⓒ Lemon grass

*Cymbopogon citratus*

see p. 71

### Ⓓ Oregano 'Hot & Spicy'

*Origanum vulgare* var. *hirtum*

see p. 102

### Ⓔ Wormwood

*Artemisia absinthium*

It doesn't have the most glamorous name, but wormwood is a useful plant. It will help repel bugs as a companion plant and can even be used to keep mosquitoes away. It's a key ingredient in traditional Moroccan mint tea, as well as a spice in making several alcoholic drinks (including absinthe). Keep it on the dry side and, even if you don't use it, you can enjoy its silvery foliage.

### Ⓕ Strawberry 'Tristar'

*Fragaria* hybrids

One of the most popular "day-neutral" strawberries in Canada, 'Tristar' doesn't wait for long days to set fruit. Expect it to bloom and yield throughout summer, though it won't send as many summer runners as the "June-bearing" types. The plant is on the small side but the fruit is sweet, plentiful and will continue right through summer. It is ideal for containers as long as it isn't allowed to dry out.

### Ⓖ Nasturtium 'Alaska Mix'

*Tropaeolum majus*

see p. 217

### Ⓗ Curry plant
*Helichrysum italicum*

Even though its smell would have you think otherwise, this plant is not an ingredient in curry, nor any other dish. It has some vague medicinal uses and has attractive foliage, but that's about it. It's edible, but the taste is very bitter. The real principle ingredient in curry is *Murraya koenigii*, commonly called masala, and looks much different.

### Ⓘ Tomato 'Tiny Tim'
*Lycopersicon lycopersicum*

Don't let the name fool you. It starts out small but, with enough heat and time, eventually grows large enough to require staking. The fruit is plentiful and decent tasting. The plant is stout, healthy and very easy to grow. Expect cherry-sized tomatoes or smaller—some ripen at just larger than a pea. It is ideal for containers or hanging baskets.

### Ⓙ Chives
*Allium schoenoprasum*

see p. 171

### Ⓚ Rosemary 'Tuscan Blue'
*Rosmarinus officinalis*

see p. 217

### Ⓛ Sage
*Salvia officinalis*

see p. 62

### Ⓜ Basil
*Ocimum basilicum*

see p. 127

### Ⓝ English thyme
*Thymus vulgaris*

Used as a battlefield antiseptic in WWI, English thyme is one of the most widely recognizable and used herbs in Canada. It's easy to grow as long as you give it lots of sun and don't overwater it. While you can use it in almost any dish, it's most popular with meats or in Mediterranean cooking. It rarely gets pests and will flourish all year if it has enough sunlight indoors.

**Height:** to 80 cm • **Spread:** to 80 cm

**MEG AND I FOUND** this design on the patio of the Teahouse restaurant in Vancouver, amongst a host of other edible containers that the restaurant used in its dishes. This container was so lush that the elements blurred into each other. Like the ferns and berries on the forest floor around the restaurant, the parts of it flowed together into a single, harmonious aesthetic.

**A** Kale 'Pigeon Red'

**B** Pineapple sage

**C** Tomato 'Tumbler'

**D** Strawberry 'Berries Galore'

**E** Leaf lettuce

**F** Italian parsley

**Recommended container size:** 70 cm across

---

The centrepiece here was a 'Pigeon Red' kale, which is listed as an ornamental kale but is just as edible as the others. The false distinction between edible and ornamental kale was made when plant breeders realized how beautiful kale could be in containers and started marketing it for that purpose.

The other ingredients are planted around the kale and weave around its broad leaves to create the interconnected look. While the red kale leaves provide a colourful centrepiece, lettuce leaves and, as they ripen, cherry tomatoes and strawberries will all add to the show.

You could easily substitute some of the lesser used ingredients, like Italian parsley and pineapple sage, for more popular basil, rosemary or even carrots and beets.

Other containers around the patio featured ferny-leafed fennel and a large rosemary for a blast of texture while fillers such as kale, lettuce and chard thrive in the temperate Vancouver

The Stanley Park Teahouse has converted the flower beds around the restaurant into beds for growing edibles for the kitchen.

weather. The restaurant uses these containers regularly, in a trend that many trendy eateries are investing in across Canada. See page 248 for more on restaurant gardens.

## Harvesting and Eating Kale

Kale's cold tolerance makes it an ideal crop for Canadian autumns. A touch of frost actually intensifies the flavour.

One of the best things about kale is its versatility. The way you use it depends on the leaves' maturity. If they are still small and immature, they're probably tender enough to use raw in salads. You'll get the most health benefits by eating them raw, and will be treated to a tantalizingly textured salad that tastes notably denser than a lettuce-based one.

Consider using the middle leaves in an Asian stir-fry. Gai lan, or Chinese broccoli, is popular throughout Asia

and is usually stir-fried with beef, but the sky is the limit. Unlike lettuce, kale is robust enough to maintain its density through the stir-frying process.

The oldest, most mature leaves are the toughest and will probably be unpalatable if eaten raw. Consider steaming these or adding them to a stew or soup where a long cooking process tenderizes them. Avoid boiling them if you're after the antioxidant benefits.

I have self-confessed salt tooth. My favourite way of eating kale is as chips. Simply cut washed and dried leaves, mature or otherwise, into bite-sized pieces. Mix them in a bowl with some olive oil and sea salt (or season to taste). Spread them on a baking sheet and cook at 350° F for 15 minutes or to desired crunchiness. They store well and are a healthier alternative to potato chips when you have a salt craving.

'Portugese' kale from Renee's Garden comes straight from Portugal and is much more heat tolerant than other varieties.

Kale chips are easy to make and one of the healthiest snacks you could ever have. These are courtesy of gardening author Alison Beck.

## ⓐ Kale 'Pigeon Red'
*Brassica oleracea* var. *acephala*

see p. 167

## ⓑ Pineapple sage
*Salvia elegans*

This native of tropical Mexico is both stately and tasty. Its edible leaves emit a fruity and exotic scent and are perfect additions to summer cocktails or any fruit dish. You'll get a miniature, though well-formed, shrub if you give it space and opportunity, but it responds well to frequent, light pinching. It's more likely to bloom indoors over winter than on your summer patio.

## ⓒ Tomato 'Tumbler'
*Lycopersicon lycopersicum*

see p. 229

## ⓓ Strawberry 'Berries Galore'
*Fragaria* hybrids

A relatively new variety bred specifically for containers, 'Berries Galore' has an attractively compact habit and fits into small pots where larger strawberry plants will just dry out. Its flowers come in downright cute shades of white, pink and red. The berries are bountiful on long runners, and terrifically sweet with a taste closer to alpine strawberries than most other varieties. Not as hardy as most, they are rated a zone 5.

## ⓔ Leaf lettuce
*Letuca sativa*

First cultivated by the ancient Egyptians, lettuce is one of the easiest and most rewarding edible crops to grow. Leaf lettuce, as opposed to head lettuce that grows like a cabbage, can be harvested anytime after the leaves are a few inches high. Keep direct seeding for a constant, fresh crop. Lettuce is high in vitamin A, fibre and calcium, and is excellent (of course) in salads.

## ⓕ Italian parsley
*Petroselinum crispum* var. *neapolitanum*

see p. 94

# THE SPICE OF MONTREAL

**Height:** to 1.5 m · **Spread:** to 1 m

**THIS BOUNTIFUL BEAUTY GREETED** me as I stepped onto the dining patio at the Montreal Botanic Garden. It's a visual *hors d'oeuvre* in a pot, making the mouth water with husky rosemary, tangy basil and peppery nasturtiums overflowing and eager to be nibbled on. The fact that edibles are most gorgeous when you want to tear them to pieces evokes the eternal question of edible gardening: to eat or not to eat.

**A** Rosemary 'Tuscan Blue'

**B** Basil 'Purple'

**C** Nasturtium 'Alaska Mix'

**D** Marigold 'Janie'

**E** Beets 'Red Ace'

**Recommended container size:**
90 cm by 90 cm

This container proves that you don't need a giant foliage ornamental to create a lush and overall gorgeous composition. Shapes, textures, colours and flavours all weave together and create tantalizing tension that beckons people over. The dilemma it poses is that its aesthetic beauty results from an overabundance of growth, which is probably destined to disappear into the kitchen.

A lot of people look at a container like this one, and especially the rosemary, and assume that it's out of their league. It's not. Woody herbs such as rosemary are ridiculously easy to keep over winter; just haul it inside and put it in a sunny spot until spring. The other ingredients here, the basil, nasturtiums and marigolds, need only heat and (the most difficult part) self-discipline to get as large as they are here.

Note the zinc container. Metal pots act as fertilizer to heat-loving edibles.

Like a solar-powered heating blanket, they heat up in the sun and keep the roots inside toasty warm. I don't recommend cool-weather veggies, like

Train your rosemary into a tree form by cutting off the lower branches, and in a few years it will be a striking specimen.

leafy greens or carrots, in these containers. Zinc is an expensive touch that, while contemporarily trendy, tends to rust if it's kept constantly wet. I'd hide a cheap fibre or plastic pot inside the zinc to keep it around longer.

## Marigolds: Natural Pest Control

Gardening is a place where knowledge and folklore can blur together to create some strange and often surprisingly effective practices. Whether or not it's best to garden by moonlight has yet to be determined, but the age-old practice of planting marigolds for natural pest prevention is now backed by science.

Every plant's internal chemistry is different, and specific plants release chemicals, whether through roots or flowers, that can be beneficial or repellent to neighbouring plants, bugs or even humans. While not a silver bullet, the scent or marigolds repels a host of nasty critters above ground and below.

Plant French marigolds (*Tagetes patula*) around members of the Solanum (Nightshade) family, which includes tomatoes, eggplant, peppers and potatoes. They are ubiquitous as the squat but pretty, perpetually cheerful, yellow and orange flowers in garden centres.

Taller marigolds with the "pom-pom" flowers (*Tagetes erecta*) are colourful statement-makers that are effective at keeping nematodes at bay. They are called Mexican, Aztec or (incorrectly) African marigolds, and include the old-fashioned but ever-popular 'Crackerjack.'

Signet marigolds (*Tagetes tenuifolia*) are the shrub-like fern-leaf types that

'Starfire' marigolds are relatively compact and bloom like crazy all summer. They also keep the pests at bay.

grow easily and create a musky scented perimeter wherever they go. Possibly the best companion plant out there, they repel aphids, whiteflies, nematodes and even mosquitoes.

---

### Ⓐ Rosemary 'Tuscan Blue'
*Rosmarinus officinalis*

Native to the Mediterranean, rosemary is a staple flavouring herb in cuisines around the world. It provides robust flavour to almost any protein dish. 'Tuscan Blue' is a stately, upright variety with sea-green foliage and profuse violet flowers. Nip off the new growth to use in your cooking, as it has the most flavour. In Canada you can bring rosemary indoors in winter to eventually grow into an impressive specimen.

### Ⓑ Basil 'Purple'
*Ocimum basilicum*

see p. 221

### Ⓒ Nasturtium 'Alaska Mix'
*Tropaeolum majus*

Nasturtiums are known for their peppery taste ("nasturtium" means "nose-twister") and no edible container should be without them. They're the easiest edible flower to grow (throw seeds into moist soil and wait), require almost no maintenance and provide months of bright colour and crisp foliage. There are scores of varieties; 'Alaska' has cream-mottled leaves that make it as ornamental as it is edible. Use the leaves and petals to garnish salads. It's even a decent source of vitamin C.

### Ⓓ Marigold 'Janie'
*Tagetes patula;* French marigold

Besides being classic, cheerful beauties in the garden, marigolds are a pest-controlling companion plant. Their roots secrete nematode-killing toxins, and whiteflies hate their smell so much that planting them next to tomatoes will keep plants whitefly free. I suggest planting one wherever you have tomatoes or peppers, for colour and for pests. Butterflies love their nectar, and the flowers bloom all summer long.

### Ⓔ Beets 'Red Ace'
*Beta vulgaris*

see p. 147

# GARDEN OF EDEN

**Height:** to 2 m • **Spread:** to 1 m

**THIS LUSH MARVEL MAKES** a real statement at the Montreal Botanic Garden's outdoor cafe. Big-volume kale and sweet potato vine bunch and squeeze together for an intense jungle aesthetic that contextualizes the centrepiece fig perfectly. The container's shameless lack of subtlety is what makes it so delicious. The plants are big, lush and irresistible.

**A** Fig 'Texas Everbearing'

**B** Basil 'Purple'

**C** Sweet potato vine 'Illusion'

**D** Papyrus 'King Tut'

**E** Marigold 'Janie'

**F** Kale 'Pigeon Red'

**G** Leaf lettuce

**Recommended container size:** 90 cm by 90 cm

The pot is designed around the 'Texas Everbearing' fig, which is the ideal variety for the long summers of Montreal. Although it grows to 5 m tall in the Mediterranean, it will probably reach around 2 m tall in a container. If you're in the market for unique edibles, and if you have a large sunny indoor space to over-winter it, a fig tree is ideal. Besides being gorgeous in its own right, it will a yield a surprising volume of fruit once it's a few years old.

To compete with the scale that the fig generates, the other ingredients need to be bulky and high on the "wow" scale. When you're dealing with over-sized centrepieces, keep in mind that accenting ingredients should maintain the same scale or the design may become lop-sided. Here, all the bulky ingredients make me feel like I've stumbled onto a giant's patio and better not get caught stealing figs.

If you're mostly interested in edible return for your dollar, this design won't work for you. The prime edible component, the fig, is pricey and some of the other plants are for ornament instead of eating. If you want this recipe to produce more, consider substituting additional kale,

You'd be amazed at the aesthetic value a few textured lettuce leaves can bring, like here mixed with violas and tomatoes.

nasturtiums, 'Pot Luck' cucumbers or even squash for the papyrus and sweet potato vine.

In the glaring sun that the other ingredients here love, the lettuce is prone to bolt and ruin. It's excellent for early and very late season flavour, but for midsummer appeal consider a heat lover such as a pepper or eggplant that will better appreciate the scorch.

## Tips for Growing Basil

Unlike some other herbs, basil is gorgeous on top of being delicious. It boasts glossy, (usually) electric green leaves and fills any space it's in with a subtle, earthy fragrance.

Watering is the key to growing basil. Keep the soil slightly moist but not soggy, and most importantly, make sure it has very good drainage. Wet feet are basil's arch-enemy, so make sure excess water isn't left in the saucer.

Put the pot in the warmest, sunniest window you have over winter. Although it's sometimes not possible to provide 6–8 hours of sunlight in winter, give as much direct light and radiant heat as possible (unless it starts to burn).

Basil appreciates a splash of fertilizer every few weeks during the growing season. If you're really keen, pick up a pH tester and check the soil to make sure it's between 6.0 and 7.5. If the pH is off, your local garden centre will know how to adjust it.

If basil is stressed it will ask for help with tell-tale yellowing leaves around the base. This usually indicates too much watering, though it can also indicate too little (its vocabulary is very limited).

There is an astonishing variety of basil available, especially in seeds from companies like Renee's Garden.

### Ⓐ Fig 'Texas Everbearing'

*Ficus carica*

see p. 102

### Ⓑ Basil 'Purple'

*Ocimum basilicum*

Dark-leaved basil tastes almost identical to the green-leaved varieties and thrives in the same conditions. The colour frightens a few people who can't imagine purple pesto; it shouldn't. In fact, the colour will add a little variety to your salad, pizza or pesto sauce. When cooking with fresh basil, add the leaves near the end of the cooking process; heat dilutes its flavour.

### Ⓒ Sweet potato vine 'Illusion'

*Ipomoea batatas*

Possibly the hottest foliage annual on the market, this heat-loving vine impresses with its bulky size and tropical flair. Although it's the same species as the sweet potato you find in stores, relentless hybridization has made its tubers, though edible, small and somewhat bitter. New short-season cultivars such as 'Georgia Jet' (110 days to maturity) are putting the real thing within reach in Canada, especially in regions with long, hot summers.

### Ⓓ Papyrus 'King Tut'

*Cyperus papyrus*

'King Tut' isn't edible, but its dynamic architecture, which is hard to find in the world of edibles, makes it a striking centrepiece to provide an aesthetic twist to your edible containers. There also a dwarf version, called 'Baby Tut,' that is handy in smaller pots. Make sure to keep it moist. The Egyptians used papyrus to make the world's first paper.

### Ⓔ Marigold 'Janie'

*Tagetes patula*

see p. 217

### Ⓕ Kale 'Pigeon Red'

*Brassica oleracea* var. *acephala*

see p. 167

### Ⓖ Leaf lettuce

*Letuca sativa*

see p. 213

# EDIBLE WINDOWSILL

**Height:** to 90 cm • **Spread:** to 80 cm

**A FEW YEARS AGO,** Meg and I visited Minter Gardens just outside of Vancouver. We were so impressed that, when this book rolled around, I called Brian Minter for a contribution. He designed this window box using a combination of classic and contemporary ingredients. He mixed unique edible flowers, like ornamental oregano, with colourful foliage and heavily producing edibles for a pot that's colourful, lush and will always bring a little something to the table.

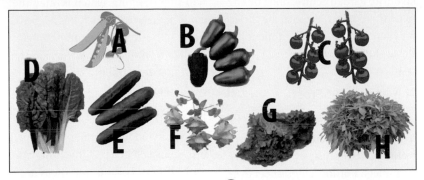

(A) Peas 'Sugar Snap'

(B) Jalapeno pepper 'Mucho Nacho'

(C) Tomato 'Tiny Tim'

(D) Swiss chard 'Bright Lights'

(E) Cucumber 'Pot Luck'

(F) Oregano 'Kent Beauty'

(G) Leaf lettuce

(H) Sweet potato vine 'Illusion'

**Recommended container size:** 30 cm by 75 cm

This container may look crowded, but it's cleverly designed to provide snacks for two seasons. During the cool nights of spring the heat-loving plants will get established but won't perform, while the peas, lettuce and chard will thrive. Once the heady days of spring give way to the dog days of summer, the cool crops will fade and even die out while the tomato, pepper, cucumber and sweet potato vine will eagerly stretch into the open spaces.

Window boxes are becoming more popular as urban gardeners find new ways to use to use the scant space available to them. In Europe, people have a massive selection of containers for metal railings and even drain-pipes. Although it's still hard to find boxes with a universal fit in Canada (i.e., will fit more than a wooden railing), the selection is getting better all the time as retailers respond to changing demands. If you don't find what you're looking for at your

'Silver Rib' is a large, striking chard that will add contemporary flair to mixed containers. It's especially good in Italian cuisine.

favourite garden centre, don't be shy to let them know. You may be the only one speaking up for a silent but eager glut of new gardeners.

## Tomatoes and Frost

Every year gardeners race against the frost, watching their green tomatoes reclining luxuriously as the mercury plummets. Putting a light sheet over the plants is a time-honoured way to cheat the first frosts (to about -3° C) of their prize. Nothing will protect tomatoes against a pending hard frost.

You can accelerate the ripening process by pruning off the top of the plant and any remaining flowers 4–6 weeks before first frost. This will force the plant to put all its remaining energy into ripening its existing fruit.

If daytime temperatures consistently drop below 15° C, the fruit typically will stop ripening, which is often the cause of the frustration. If this happens, harvest the green tomatoes that have slightly translucent flesh (less along than that are harder to ripen) and bring them inside.

It's a myth that exposure to sunlight speeds up indoor ripening. They need only consistent heat with a hint of ethylene gas. For this, put them in a paper bag with a little chopped apple or a banana peel. The bag will act as a mini greenhouse, raising the humidity and temperature.

Tomatoes use oxygen stored in their vines to ripen, so the more vine you leave on, the better. If the plant is still full of green tomatoes and a hard frost is pending, uproot the entire plant (or a sizeable portion) and hang it upside down in a dark place. You'll be surprised how many tomatoes will ripen.

There's a rainbow of beefy, colourful heirloom tomatoes to choose from, so don't be afraid to think outside the red.

### Ⓐ Peas 'Sugar Snap'
*Pisum sativum;* snap peas

Peas are virtually maintenance free once the trellis is in place, or you can just let them trail over the side of the container. They love cool weather and tend to stop producing in summer but will pick up again in fall. Enjoy snap peas' edible pods raw or cook them in stir-fries.

### Ⓑ Jalapeno pepper 'Mucho Nacho'
*Capsicum annuum*

see p. 186

### Ⓒ Tomato 'Tiny Tim'
*Lycopersicon lycopersicum*

see p. 209

### Ⓓ Swiss chard 'Bright Lights'
*Beta vulgaris* subsp. *cicla;* silverbeet

Chard is related to beets, but years of breeding for better tasting/healthier leaves have led to a reduced tuber. It is an excellent source of vitamins C and K, and antioxidants. Its bright colours add vibrancy to edible containers. Chard is a cool-weather crop for spring and fall.

### Ⓔ Cucumber 'Pot Luck'
*Cucumis sativus*

see p. 119

### Ⓕ Oregano 'Kent Beauty'
*Origanum rotundifolium*

'Kent Beauty' doesn't have nearly the same taste as other oregano varieties. What is does have are gorgeous pink-tinged bracts and crisp blue-green leaves. It's a great addition to mixed edible containers, or plant it by itself in a hanging basket. Try the bracts as long-lasting cut flowers in arrangements.

### Ⓖ Leaf lettuce
*Letuca sativa*

see p. 213

### Ⓗ Sweet potato vine 'Illusion'
*Ipomoea batatas*

see p. 221

# BERRIES AND LACE

**Height:** to 1 m • **Spread:** to 90 cm

**EDIBLE PLANTS TEND TO BE** robust, sturdy plants with a squat centre of gravity. This container, designed by Brian Minter of Minter Gardens just outside Vancouver, offers a buoyant and light-hearted addition to a heavy crowd. Ferny fennel leaves, upward arching oregano bracts, and floating geranium flowers give this design a feminine grace.

Ⓐ Fennel

Ⓑ Strawberry 'Berries Galore'

Ⓒ Oregano 'Kent Beauty'

Ⓓ Rose geranium

Ⓔ Parsley 'Triple Curled'

Ⓕ Raspberry 'Autumn Bliss'

Ⓖ Tomato 'Tumbler'

Ⓗ Rosemary 'Tuscan Blue'

**Recommended container size:** 60–80 cm across

Fennel is such a striking centrepiece that it's too bad it's not a more popular edible. Whether green or bronze, its delicate leaves bring a refreshing contrast to the broad dark greens of tomatoes and cucumbers. If you want to do more with gentle textures, try combining fennel, carrots, dill, calendula, thyme and even curled parsley. You could place it across the doorway from a broad-leafed blend of cucumbers, nasturtiums, basil and kale for a stark, pan-threshold contrast.

As always with edible container gardening, you'll need to strike your own balance between usefulness and aesthetics. You'll want to figure out how much you want to look at it versus eat it. Besides the beautiful fennel and ornamental oregano, Brian has plenty for the kitchen. He planted the prolific 'Tumbler' tomato next to strawberries and raspberries. At the end of the season, you may want to move the raspberry to the centre of the pot for overwintering.

If you like the oregano and want to add more colour, consider pansies, nasturtiums and calendula around the fennel to make an edible flower collage.

Ferny-leafed fennel looks striking in the centre of this container surrounded by a simple nest of lysimachia.

## Growing Raspberries in Containers

There's absolutely no comparison to fresh garden raspberries. Although they are one of the most popular edibles to grow in Canada, not many people associate them with container gardening. That's all changing.

Traditionally, raspberries have followed a two-year growth cycle wherein the primocanes (suckers) grow the first year but don't fruit. It's only the next

If you have a big container, don't be afraid to grow raspberry canes. All you should need is a little wrapping around the pot in winter.

year, when they graduate to floricane status, that they start to yield. After the floricanes fruit, they die and a fresh crop of suckers prepares to set fruit. The complex, multi-year cycle of these "summer" raspberries makes them well-suited for garden patches.

The "everbearing" or "autumn" raspberry is becoming exponentially more popular as gardeners move their edibles to containers. It yields on the primocanes (that season's growth). The fruit comes later than summer-bearing types but is just as delicious. In the very early spring, before the new sprouts appear, cut the canes down to the ground to make way for that year's crop.

You'll need a large container, as raspberries still need to overwinter. Try putting them in the centre of a large pot and planting annual edibles, such as your favourite herbs, around them. Make sure to keep them moist, especially during heat waves. They appreciate a little fertilizer and slightly acidic soils (I use a peat moss based medium). Don't forget to mix some yummy compost into the soil.

**ⓐ Fennel**
*Foeniculum vulgare*

see p. 78

**ⓑ Strawberry 'Berries Galore'**
*Fragaria* hybrids

see p. 213

### ⓒ Oregano 'Kent Beauty'
*Origanum rotundifolium*

see p. 225

### ⓓ Rose geranium
*Pelargonium graveolens*

One of the oldest bedding plants out there is making a comeback. Old-school geraniums may not bloom as much as their modern, hyper-hybridized cousins, but what they lack in colour they make up for in style. They boast triangular leaves with dark red colouration on them. The tea makes an excellent anti-depressant.

### ⓔ Parsley 'Triple Curled'
*Petroselinum crispum*

see p. 171

### ⓕ Raspberry 'Autumn Bliss'
*Rubus idaeus*

The type of raspberry you choose for your container will depend largely on your climate zone. 'Autumn Bliss' is a reliable autumn bearer that yields from late August on. Its well-behaved, somewhat compact canes make it ideal for containers. The fruit is large and tasty and freezes well. In colder regions, try 'Heritage.'

### ⓖ Tomato 'Tumbler'
*Lycopersicon lycopersicum*

'Tumbler' was bred to thrive in containers, especially hanging baskets, where it can hang over the edge and produce buckets of fruit. It's a determinate tomato that won't grow overly large, but each plant should produce about 2 kg of 2–4 cm wide, sweet tomatoes per season. Make sure to keep it well watered (mulch helps) and well fertilized. The best way to eat these tomatoes is straight from the garden.

### ⓗ Rosemary 'Tuscan Blue'
*Rosmarinus officinalis*

see p. 217

# MAKING FRESH FOOD ACCESSIBLE IN TORONTO

Don't be afraid to blend different colours and textures of salad greens together for a richer display.

**I WANTED TO FIND** people and projects in Canada where edible gardening was being used in innovative ways. Knowing that one of the features needed to focus on the exploding popularity of community gardening, I started looking for the most exciting community gardens in the country. My search didn't last long; all signs pointed to Toronto.

A drip watering ball set amongst the sage makes sure it gets a slow and constant supply of water during hot Toronto summers.

I set off to the hustle-bustle of our largest city to see its community gardens. I was prepared to be impressed, but the passion, ambition and results of the project I found left me dizzyingly inspired. Before I get into the details of the project and its gardens, a little context.

## Food Deserts

The geography of Canadian cities is changing. City centres that were once home to small grocery stores are being hollowed out as a combination of suburbanization and commercial concentration is focusing retailers into larger centres on the outskirts of town. In an increasing number of cities, residents living near the core, and who can't afford vehicles, face a public transit odyssey just to access healthy, fresh food. These inner city areas are known as "food deserts," and they are a growing problem in Canada.

FoodShare Headquarters doubles as a community garden and buzzes with enthusiasm and activity.

People who live inside food deserts tend to have below average household incomes and often live in racialized communities. Limited access to fresh food causes a host of social and health problems. While many of us don't like to think that malnutrition can exist in the hearts of our most iconic cities, the truth is that it certainly does; we just don't always see it. Cities are some of the most isolating places there are.

## FoodShare Toronto

FoodShare Toronto is a non-profit community organization brimming with passionate people brought together by the vision of providing "Good Healthy Food for All," and they get results. As Canada's largest community food security organization, they reach over 145,000 children and adults a month through subsidized fresh food programs, community gardening and cooking, classroom curriculum support, homemade baby food workshops and youth internships.

FoodShare takes a holistic approach to urban food security, emphasizing "teaching people how to fish" to create a sustainable capacity building model. They stress education and community cooperation, knowing that creating linkages between neighbours is the crucial first step toward growing their own food. Community building, which happens when neighbours get to know each other, is at the heart of these gardens.

Although the community gardens I focused on are a very narrow aspect of FoodShare's overall operation, I was profoundly impressed by their ability to blend productivity and passion into a model with the gravitas to inspire community groups across Canada for years ahead.

Planters at Brock Public School are shaped like honeycombs to help teach children about the importance of pollinating insects.

## Brock Public School

I drove east from downtown, fighting Toronto's legendary traffic, not knowing what the day had in store. I found Mary Roufail at her outside "office," namely a well-used picnic table in the middle of the thriving gardens outside the FoodShare offices. Mary works at FoodShare as a community food animation coordinator. They use the term "animate" because they facilitate connections between people, a spark that creates motion, motivation and cooperation where before there was stagnancy.

The first thing I noticed was the relatively young age of the people there and their personal comfort with each other. I immediately saw that it was a unique workplace environment where people were brought together by the unspoken understanding that

Corn is planted in full exposure inside a black, metallic window box that will soak up the sun and accelerate growth for a bigger harvest.

they all worked for the same cause, and I quickly felt at ease.

FoodShare is a grassroots organization that works from within the community, not above it. They partner with dozens of community gardens in low-income areas throughout Toronto. Many of the gardens are in food deserts and stand as bastions of nutritious food and growing awareness in their communities.

Tomatoes and peas are planted in simple, affordable, homemade self-watering containers made of two 5-gallon buckets.

We walked to the Brock Terrace Garden, which was built on the third storey balcony of nearby Brock Public School. Part of FoodShare's "Field to Table Schools" program, the garden was designed as much as an educational tool as a community garden. The elementary school uses it to teach urban kids about the benefits of growing and eating fresh food.

Like many urban schools across Canada, the halls of Brock tell the story of teachers and parents going an extra mile, and then another and another, to stretch very limited resources. Paint-peeling walls are adorned with rows of bright, motivational posters and well-loved projects. There's so much hope for the future here that it has seeped into the walls, windows and cubby holes.

The advantages to growing tomatoes upside down are that they don't grow in the dirt and enjoy excellent air circulation.

Some simple row cover over your garden or raised beds will keep out voracious, egg-laying flying insects like cabbage moths.

The terrace sprawls across the third floor and overlooks the east side of downtown all the way to the CN Tower. I notice the colours right away. One side of the wooden terrace is dedicated to blue wading-pool planters arranged in a honeycomb pattern. FoodShare staff member Justin Nadeau, who designed the garden, created the look to teach kids about the relationship between bees and food.

In the centre of the terrace, surrounded a sheltered seating area, are bright red and green buckets full of tomatoes, beans, peas and cucumbers. There's corn, upside-down tomatoes and raised beds that look like covered wagons with their green mesh tops. It's a garden built to grow a child's imagination as much as food, and the kids love it.

Every garden should have at least one composter, and there are many models with almost no smell.

## Dragon Alley

A short walk away from Brock Public School lies an exciting garden that is blurring the boundaries between guerrilla and community gardening. Tucked between rows of housing covered in graffiti, Dragon Alley was once as neglected as a back alley can be. Kids played in a crumbling cinder block garage surrounded by heaps of hazards and garbage. What's happened since is a dramatic example of how a few neighbours can animate a community and turn chaos into growth.

The garden is a relatively new project. A few years ago, the alley (the name "Dragon" came later) was derelict and a dangerous place for children. Cheryl Douglass, a concerned resident, got fed up one day and started filling garbage bags with the garbage strewn about. To her surprise, when she went back the next morning another neighbour had silently stepped in to throw them out.

There are many simple and affordable, or free, found materials that you can use to define the borders of a vegetable bed.

The initial, unsolicited spark of cooperation continued to grow as more people got involved. Residents from ages four to 85 all pitched in, making the alley a safer place to play

The garden's positon at either end of a parking lot makes it an original model of space sharing that I hope will be replicated elsewhere.

The Dragon Alley garden owes its existence to the creative perseverance of Cheryl Douglass (left) and Sophia Ilyniak (right).

When you start looking for creative found materials to use as planters and in your edible gardens, you will find them everywhere.

by sweeping it regularly. It became a parking lot owned by the Toronto Parking Authority (TPA). At that point Sophia Ilyniak, a student at Ontario College of Art and Design, and her roommates started planting edibles in the lot's bordering areas to create a welcoming environment. Both children and adults joined in and, as the garden grew, tables and chairs were added to develop a communal meeting place.

Cheryl explained the origin of the name as a tribute to the women who conceived and maintain the garden. In myth, dragons are often strong female figures. Growing edibles in a space this unusual was a first in the city, and it stirred up a negotiation process between the gardeners and the TPA. Aided by FoodShare and supportive councillors like Ana Bailão, who put forth the motion to name it "Dragon Alley," the residents held firm to their vision of a food garden and gathering place. The TPA provided key support and installed planter boxes at both ends of the lot. When I visited in summer 2012, Dragon Alley, FoodShare and the TPA were finalizing legal agreements to formalize their roles and expectations.

Dragon Alley community garden lies at either end of the parking lot that dominates most of the space. The garden is multi-faceted and well-loved, with areas where neighbours can gather to relax, a sacred plants garden, a compost bin, and a host of vegetables and herbs planted throughout. Residents are steadily taking more ownership as they plant, maintain and love the garden. With each volunteer hour, the community is defining Dragon Alley's future and elevating a neglected back alley into something inspiring.

The city built a wooden planter in the garden that the neighbours have filled with leafy greens and herbs.

You don't have to spend a lot of money to have useful garden accessories. This old bicycle tire makes an ideal trellis for climbing vines.

Jeanny Gonzalez looks after the Rockford garden and is proud that local families have the chance to grow hard-to-find varieties of food.

## Rockford Community Garden

I met with Jeanny Gonzalez to look at the Rockford Community Garden in the neighbourhood of Bathurst and Finch. A classic food desert, this neighbourhood is largely made up of low-income, immigrant families, and for those without a vehicle, access to fresh food is difficult at best.

Unlike Brock Public School and Dragon Alley, Rockford looks like a traditional community garden. There are 20 well-kept and well-loved family plots where local families plant an astonishing amount of fresh food in the small space they have. Using creative space-saving techniques, they've made a bountiful garden that provides them with

The Rockford garden plots are each tended by a different family or individual, and they are all meticulously maintained.

a steady trickle of fresh food through-out summer. Many families use the space to plant vegetables and herbs from their native countries, which would be almost impossible for them to access otherwise but are an integral part of their culinary culture.

Gardens such as Rockford are as unsettling as they are inspiring. While they demonstrate the tenacity of people wanting to empower themselves by growing their own food, they also

highlight the magnitude of a problem that many Canadians are still surprised to learn about.

In Toronto I learned that we have a long way to go before all Canadians have access to fresh, nutritious food. At the same time, I saw how far a small group of dedicated people can go toward solving the problem. You can learn more about their vision, and how you can get involved, at www.foodshare.net.

The garden makes excellent use of a field adjacent to a school.

# MCGILL UNIVERSITY ROOFTOP GARDENS

The team used easy-to-build, affordable self-watering containers. The design is available at www.archives.rooftopgardens.ca

**WHEN WE TALK** about growing food in containers, we're usually talking about how we optimize space. As record amounts of Canadians move into cities, more people are being condensed into the same amount of space. This army of city dwellers, refusing to let the lack of a backyard stop them from growing fresh food for themselves and their families, are the beating heart of the grow-your-own movement. Many of the innovations

The Rooftop Gardens Project team has set up across post-secondary institutions across Montreal.

we've seen in the past few years, from vertical gardening to compact vegetable varieties, have been about growing more food in less space.

In Montreal I learned to take a second look at urban spaces and their potential. While gardening can empower communities and bring people together, it traditionally happens on privately owned space. You may trade zucchini for potatoes with your neighbour, but both of you grew them in your own yards.

I travelled to the vibrant city of Montreal because when I asked people across Canada about exciting edible gardening projects, they inevitably said, "Have you been to McGill?" When I got there, I learned how growing fresh food in institutional public spaces, as opposed to private residential spaces, can become a beacon for broad social change. At one of the country's most iconic institutions, I saw how the concrete cores of cities could be transformed for the benefit of all residents.

Hundreds of containers add life and a sense of vitality to an otherwise sedate concrete walkway.

Large cloth bags set into simple metal frames is an easy and affordable way to make your own edible containers.

## The Rooftop Gardens Project

Alternatives International isn't a group that you'd normally associate with gardening. Active in 35 countries, they spearhead initiatives that bring people together to stand for

This multi-tiered tower consists of simple metal frames lined with landscape fabric. The plants grow out of slits in the fabric.

environmental and human rights issues. When I stepped into their Montreal office, I didn't understand why a group like this would be interested in container-grown edibles. When I learned about their projects and realized the interconnections between social change and gardening, it made my head spin.

Gaëlle Janvier met me on a bike and took me into the heart of the storied McGill campus to show me one of the spaces the Rooftop Gardens Project had participated in reclaiming. A partnership between Alternatives and Montreal-based Santropol Roulant, the goal of the project is, in Gaëlle's words, "to build gardeners and for people to reconnect with their food as a community." It's about educating and empowering people to take control of their own food sovereignty.

You don't need to spend a fortune on containers to produce scores of vegetables.

Eager to pull edible gardening out of peoples' backyards and into the openness of public city spaces, the Rooftop Gardens Project and Santropol Meals on Wheels, in partnership with the Santropol food bank, chose McGill for its hyper-institutionalized reputation. The garden transforms and reclaims a part of the McGill campus into a collective and productive space.

It was first established in 2007. Like the FoodShare gardens in Toronto, it started with a very few people connecting with each other and animating others. Although hesitant at first, McGill now recognizes the benefits of the project and actively promotes it with funding. In creating a collective space, the garden enriches the campus and benefits all parties. I hope that word of how well it's working will spread across Canada.

In 2012, the Santropol Roulant team planted about 200 edible containers at McGill and plans to give 2 tons of fresh produce to the Santropol food bank. Most of it goes to elderly people or those with limited mobility who

These homemade self-watering containers come with a watering tube to make it even easier.

Beans are voracious climbers and only need sturdy string to climb as long as it has knots or horizontal cross-overs to provide leverage.

might not otherwise have access to fresh food.

With the garden in such a high-traffic and public area, I asked if theft was a major issue. Gaëlle said that besides not being able to grow certain plants, like tomatoes, in the busiest pedestrian areas, there was only minor theft of food.

The Edible Campus stretches over several rooftops, down main thoroughfares, through central meeting points

By the end of summer these cucumbers will cover this arch and the fruit will hang below the mesh, out of the dirt and ready to be picked.

and even climbs up buildings. It was inspiring to see how bare concrete could be transformed into a productive, enriching, oxygenating space. Students studied, hustled, chatted and relaxed among the containers, used to the garden as being a part of their post-secondary landscape.

The designers made excellent use of companion planting. Marigolds abound, providing passive, ongoing pest prevention and colour. Basil thrives alongside peppers and tomatoes, while fennel, being an infamously nasty container-mate, grows alone.

Margiolds are ideal companion plants for peppers, and add a splash of summer colour as a bonus.

There's also an effective use of vertical gardening. Beans climb long ropes that drop down the wall of an over-sized staircase. On top of that, cucumbers are trained on wooden stakes to create a tunnel through two rows of containers. Back at ground level, beans and peppers are supported by rope and wood along a massive concrete building with western exposure.

The vegetable fennel produces an edible bulb at its base while the herb fennel is grown for its foliage and seeds.

A large bed, complete with row-cover tunnels to keep the flying pests at bay, completes the McGill project.

For edibles that are harder to grow in containers, such as garlic, there is a large planted bed. There are rows of Swiss chard, safely protected from bugs under mesh screening, and strawberries surrounded by golden straw to prevent the berries from rotting as they ripen.

If you look at a city from the sky, the phrase "concrete jungle" comes into unsettling focus. The lack of vegetation in large urban centres causes them to be several degrees hotter than the surrounding countryside. Urban gardens and agriculture, like the Edible Campus, help cool the air, add oxygen and make cities healthier for the citizens.

At the same time, heat-loving plants such as tomatoes, peppers and eggplants thrive in the furnace of the inner city.

Empowerment through education is at the heart of the McGill project. By defining institutional rooftops and sidewalks as space to grow food, the team is seeking to inspire people to learn how to grow food of their own in non-traditional spaces.

Now that this garden is established and running on its own, Gaëlle tells me that Alternatives' emphasis has shifted toward education and supporting other organizations in their efforts to develop gardens. The group has published an 80-page online book with specific lesson plans and objectives for teachers interested in teaching their class about the importance of fresh food. The pedagogical guide "Roots Around the World" is available for free.

Walking away from McGill, the confusion I felt in the Alternatives office a few hours before was gone. It made perfect sense that a human rights group would be interested in edible container gardening. The ability to grow your own food is a powerfully self-actualizing skill that, unfortunately, has become scarce in recent history. People with access to fresh produce tend to be more community oriented, healthier, and more thoughtful about environmental issues that affect the planet.

Rooftop gardeners across Montreal enjoy gorgeous views and ideal growing temperatures.

McGill is only one part of the Rooftop Gardens Project. Alternatives also supports groups in Haiti as they develop gardens in schools and shanty towns, and in Cameroon for subsistence urban farming strategies. They are dedicated to promoting food awareness and sovereignty worldwide, no matter what the type of food is. To learn more about the projects and how you can get involved, go to www.alternatives.ca.

Simple wooden supports connected by sturdy string is all you need for an overhanging garden.

# THE RISE OF LOCALLY GROWN EDIBLES IN RESTAURANTS

The Royal York rooftop garden might just have the best view of any edible garden in Canada.

**CANADIANS ARE BECOMING** more curious and critical about the ingredients behind restaurant menus. The explosion in popularity of home-grown edibles, coupled with celebrity chefs like Gordon Ramsay and Jamie Oliver preaching the doctrine that fresh ingredients are at the heart of great food, have made questioning the genealogy of the basil and broccoli on our plates the norm.

An increasing number of restaurants, typically higher-end, are opting to establish a niche with people who will pay a little more for locally sourced ingredients. Veggie beds and herb planters are sprouting up around the patios and back doors of restaurants across Canada, and chefs are using the opportunity to express their creativity with a new level of freshness.

## Leaf & Lyre, Calgary

When you drive down city streets and see edibles spilling out of containers and raised beds in peoples' yards, they aren't always for the reason you think. With their unique business model, Chad Kile and his partner Rod Olson of Leaf & Lyre Urban Farms have taken an innovative approach to urban agriculture wherein they plant lettuce, kale, arugula, spinach, beets and more in 20 donated home gardens across Calgary. Multiple city-centre

restaurants snatch up their crops, eager for an increased supply of locally grown produce.

When I asked him why eateries are so interested in local edibles, Chad tells me that motivations are both philosophical and political. "They [the chefs] are food artists for whom excellent vegetables are an aesthetic virtue, and these come from a healthy local food industry in which food producers are similarly passionate about the quality of the produce they offer."

Leaf & Lyre uses raised beds like this one (above) across Calgary to grow leafy greens (below) for popular downtown restaurants.

## The Teahouse, Vancouver

Whenever my wife and I are in Vancouver, we make sure to take a turn around the Seawall rimming Stanley Park. We mark the end of one of Canada's best walks with a visit to the Teahouse, one of our favourite restaurants and perched above English Bay with a commanding view of the ocean beyond.

The last time we were there, we noticed that the customary ornamental container gardens had been replaced with pots of herbs, vegetables and berries. Customers ate their lunch surrounded by fresh ingredients, some of which were on their plates. I chatted with executive chef Annabelle Leslie, and she explained that the containers were a simple, reliably pesticide-free way to offset food costs. Cherry tomatoes, herbs, bay leaves, kale and fennel all found their way into the Teahouse kitchen. I was so impressed with the artistry of the designs that I featured one of them, "In Stanley Park," on page 210.

Texture and shape play as big a role in edible containers as colour does in ornamental containers.

Bees from the Vancouver Fairmont apiary pollinate most of downtown Vancouver.

## Fairmont Waterfront, Vancouver

The Canadian industry leader for providing locally sourced herbs and vegetables to their customers is the Fairmont chain of hotels. Fairmont chefs take the term "local" to the extreme by building extensive gardens on the hotel roofs and grounds. In Vancouver, we toured the 2100-square-foot herb garden at the Fairmont Waterfront, with its commanding views of the harbour and North Vancouver. The garden was Vancouver's first green roof when it was built in 1991 and is home to 60 varieties of edibles, a dozen species of birds and a whole lot of bees.

Being in the heart of the city, the chefs at the Waterfront confronted a problem that is becoming unsettlingly common across Canada: pollinators are scarce. To rectify this, they installed an apiary and established their own

honeybee population. We watched as the bees hovered and buzzed about the hives, coming and going with their morsels of hard-earned nectar. The half-million resident bees have to visit a million flowers in order to produce one pound of honey. Given that the hotel's annual Honey Harvest brings in about 600 pounds of honey,

The beehives are painted to blend in with the surrounding gardens.

the busy bees must have graced 600,000,000 flowers!

Our guide, Michael King, explained that having the bees benefits a wide area around the hotel as they search far and wide for those 600,000,000 blooms. They pollinate high-rise balconies, boulevard flowers and fruiting trees as far away as Stanley Park and North Vancouver, in a staggering 40-kilometre radius around the hotel. Honey from different times of the season tastes slightly different, depending on the flowers that happen to be in bloom.

The next morning over breakfast, I smiled when a small jar of Waterfront honey appeared at our table. While much of the honey is used in the restaurant, it's also given away and sold.

Well-groomed boxwood hedges create attractive borders for the rooftop herbs and veggie beds.

## Fairmont Royal York, Toronto

I heard rave reviews about the jewel of Canada's herb gardens, which was built atop one of Canada's most iconic hotels, the Fairmont Royal York in Toronto. Public relations coordinator Catherine Tschannen organized a tour with executive sous chef Andrew Court on a hot July morning.

The garden consists of 16 large raised beds and made the Royal York a rooftop gardening pioneer when it was constructed in 1998. It's open to the public for tours on summer weekends. It has none of the pomp and circumstance of the hotel's public façade. The beds are simple and utilitarian and the plants are healthy, well cared for and well used. There are dozens of different plants grown, and almost all of them are earmarked for specific dishes.

The CN Tower looms over the Royal York's 16 elevated wooden beds.

An attractive and useful archway welcomes visitors to the Royal York gardens.

Executive Sous Chef Andrew Court beams when he talks about what the rooftop garden has done for quality and authenticity in the hotel restaurants.

Most of the herbs in the garden end up in the Royal York's flagship restaurant, EPIC, which advertises that every dish contains rooftop ingredients. The restaurant's style is contemporary and unabashedly local. Chefs create dishes such as "Exotic Ontario Mushroom Ravioli" and "Foraged Canadian Wild Ginger Crème Brûlèe" by finding new ways to use fresh elements. The demands of a restaurant like EPIC, which doesn't shy away from hard-to-find ingredients, have necessitated that portions of the rooftop garden be allocated to plants such as the surprisingly spicy 'Wasabi' arugula,

Hard-to-find varieties of Asian and Turkish eggplant grow throughout the garden.

alpine strawberries and 'Red Genovese' basil to ensure a reliable supply. While the easy-to-find 'Amethyst' eggplant is nowhere to be found, rare varieties such as 'Kurume Long,' 'Thai Purple Blush' and 'Turkish Orange' brandish their strange fruit. While the common curly kale is absent, 'Tuscan Black,' a purist Mediterranean favourite, is planted in abundance.

Chef Court tells me that the number of ethnic culinary plants reflects the hotel's desire to cater to visitors from

The garden ensures consistent availability and quality of hard-to-find gourmet veggies like this striking 'Redbor' kale

The Royal York restaurants serve wasabi for sushi the traditional way, on a leaf of fresh green shiso.

Edible flowers like violas are popular in restaurant desserts and during afternoon tea. They grow beautifully in the shade of Swiss chard.

There are rows of pansies and other edible flowers for afternoon tea and a host of herbs earmarked for desserts and drinks. From pineapple sage to an entire bed full of 'Mohito' mint, the plants are a required staple of many popular menu items.

Being in the heart of the city, the hotel also boasts a 300,000-strong honey-bee apiary, which produced about 800 pounds of honey in 2011. The sweet stuff finds its way into salad dressings, teas, pastries or ice cream, or it is given away to special guests.

When I asked Chef Court what he believes was the catalyst for people's increasing desire for local foods, he took a generational perspective that's becoming familiar when I ask people to reflect on the home-grown movement. Court said that most visitors to the garden are couples in their 30s to 50s, often with children tagging close behind. "For a generation that was lost [in the 1950s and 60s],

around the world. A steady supply of green shiso (for Benihara Teppanyaki Restaurant and Sushi Bar) is tough to secure in Canada but, because wasabi is traditionally served on its leaves, the hotel needed to find a way to be "authentic to the original."

Climbing nasturtiums and rare burgundy okra grow unmolested by pests thanks to the yellow tagetes marigolds.

convenience food was huge. Families weren't sitting down eating and cooking together. Convenience food has been there and gone. Families want to come back together, and the kitchen table is the best place to do that."

Court cites the farm-to-fork movement (also called farm-to-table). This movement was founded on the premise that food is safer and local farming is more sustainable when producers and restaurants form a closer relationship. In the case of EPIC and other restaurants across Canada, food is sourced as locally as possible, even if that means building a rooftop garden to ensure the supply.

Farm-to-fork advocates are heavily invested in educating people about where fresh food comes from, what farming communities put into producing it, and the many ways it can be used and misused before it's eaten. Just like Jamie Oliver's "Food Revolution" is based on the belief that the best weapon against obesity is teaching kids where their food comes from and what good food looks, feels and tastes like, farm-to-fork is about prioritizing

local producers in the hopes of stemming the dominance of genetically modified foods and an increasingly centralized food supply system.

Court says that the Royal York uses the garden to train apprentice chefs and allow them to hone their craft on the same ingredients the restaurant uses. "They see how tomatillos are grown, and they experiment and develop dishes for them."

Over a dozen containers add doses of other edibles, like lemon grass surrounded by tagetes marigolds.

This entire bed consists of 'Mohito' mint for one of the bar's favourite cocktails.

# EDMONTON VALLEY ZOO ENRICHMENT GARDEN

Squash and pumpkins overflow their bed at the Edmonton Valley Zoo Enrichment Garden.

**MOST OF THIS BOOK** has been about how edible gardening benefits humans. As an avid animal lover, I didn't want to leave out the rest of the earth's population.

My wife and I love the Edmonton Valley Zoo and are on a first-name basis with many of the fauna strutting, flapping and hopping around the enclosures. After my Masters' degree defence, Meg soothed my jangled nerves by taking me to the watch the zoo's prairie dogs burrow, wrestle and squeak.

In early spring 2012, she encouraged me to reach out the zoo to see if they were interested in cooperating with my garden centre, Salisbury Greenhouse, on a project. I didn't know what they'd be interested in doing or even if I'd get a call back, but to my delight Barbara Chapman, vice-president of the Valley Zoo Development Society, rebutted my abstract offer with a concrete proposal. She wanted to install an enrichment garden at the zoo, and without even knowing what that was, I signed up.

Salisbury Greenhouse partnered with Shignanski Construction to build the raised beds.

The term "enrichment," in its broadest sense as it applies to zoos, is about giving animals access to objects that promote mental and physical health. These could be toys to promote mental acuity, sensory objects to activate ears and noses, or dietary supplements that have health and/or behavioural benefits. The latter is where Salisbury came in.

Animals enjoy the increased nutrients in home-grown veggies just like humans do. Fresh edibles also promote play and puzzle solving in some animals, like the zoo's snow leopard, who loves to shuck corn. I went into the project thinking that I was helping to build a garden simply to supplement the animals' diet. When I realized what the garden was really for, it became one of the most satisfying projects I've ever worked on.

I partnered with Justin Shignanski of Shignanski Construction to build the

planters. With it being a temporary project, he built 10 untreated spruce planters, each 10 feet by 4 feet for 400 square feet of growing space. The volunteer-driven Valley Zoo Development Society, with their mandate of developing and enhancing the zoo and the animals, was immensely helpful. Barbara, who remained passionately driven throughout the project, mustered a wish-list of plants from the zookeepers that included everything from pumpkins

The garden produces hundreds of pounds of veggies, fruit and herbs for the zoo animals to eat and engage with.

to yarrow to pansies. We brought in topsoil and mixed it with "zoo-poo," much of which had been generously donated by the resident elephant, Lucy. Salisbury provided the plants and, thanks to a host of volunteers brought in by Telus to help plant, we were on our way.

When I visited the garden in late August, they were harvesting gallons of tomatoes every second day and soccer ball–sized squash and pumpkins were hanging heavy on the vines. It was a massive success, with keepers standing in line for choice plants for their eager animals. I started getting suggestions and notes for next years' plants right away, and I am grateful that Meg prodded me to make that first tentative phone call. It makes me think of the word that they use at FoodShare Toronto, "animate." Every great project starts with an initial spark, a connection between people that just happens to be in the right place at the right time.

The author plucking some purple fountain grass from one of the beds.

The ring-tailed lemurs jumped over each other to get at the fresh corn.

## Close Encounters

The staff at the zoo invited me and photographer Megan Mundell-Hahn in for a behind the scenes look at how the animals engaged with the plants. With Barbara and a series of zookeepers and supervisors as our guides, we went from enclosure to enclosure and were amazed at what we saw. It was a once in a lifetime chance to see the animals up close and personal and how the project enriched their lives. I'll never forget it.

We started with the ring-tailed lemurs. They scampered over to us and greedily devoured corn cob pieces, clutching them deftly with both hands as they jostled with each other for the best bits. The red lemurs were more assertive, climbing up our legs and grabbing at the camera in their search for snacks.

The red lemurs were curious enough to make a grab at my camera to see if it was food.

Needles the porcupine was too hot that afternoon to enjoy his favourite edible flowers, but he enjoyed them later.

Pip the red panda loves fresh fruit and isn't shy about tugging at your leg to see if you have more.

The two North American porcupines, appropriately named Pins and Needles, were considerably more mellow. Normally big fans of the fresh strawberries and pansy flowers, they preferred to lie in the shade through the afternoon heat.

Next on the tour was Pip, an endangered red panda that the zoo cares for as part of the Species Survival Plan. Pip started out shy but, once presented with fresh apples, threw timidity to the wind and munched happily, holding the fruit in her snow-shoe paws up to her unforgettable teddy-bear face.

Zookeeper Greg Lalonde beamed with pride as he introduced Newton, a very rare New Zealand kea, a type of parrot. Still a youngster, Newton is the first kea ever to hatch successfully in captivity in Canada. He's a sucker for texture, rolling in fountain grass plumes and rubbing his body against fuzzy lamb's ear.

Newton is a very rare New Zealand kea who loves the texture of fountain grass and lamb's ear (above and below).

The next animal we visited needs no introduction. Lucy the elephant is iconic at the zoo for her gentle manner and artistic talent. Lucy loves sweets but, for weight management reasons, she's not allowed to have them. We planted a pot of stevia, a 0-calorie sugar substitute, in the garden just for her. I felt a lump of emotion in my throat as she hungrily ate a handful of it, finally able once again to eat the sweet treats she loves.

Lucy loves her stevia!

As we moved on to the carnivores, I began to understand how enrichment means so much more than food. When we walked into the Amur (Siberian) tiger enclosure, my heart quickened. With only a steel fence between us, I was standing a few feet away from the largest cats in the world, cats I had been fascinated by as a child and who looked at me like a tenderloin fresh off the barbecue.

When zookeeper Robyn Kunimoto gave them pumpkins from the enrichment garden, they turned into kittens again, running around the enclosure and leaping over them. With the squash held helplessly in their paws, they stretched their mouths around it and happily tore it to shreds as they played.

The last stop was to see Shilah and Kayok, the Arctic wolves. Supervisor Wade Krasnow rubbed lavender leaves on a rock, and the wolves happily rubbed themselves in it to disguise their scent. I was amazed, having had no idea that the carnivores would have anything to do with the garden edibles.

The plants were so diverse, and the keepers so creative in how they used them, that virtually every fuzzy, feathery, leathery and scaly zoo resident engaged with them in some way.

Tigers may play just like kittens, but they look at you like they wish you were lunch.

# INDEX

Names in **boldface** refer to designs; page numbers in **boldface** refer to full plant descriptions.

# ABOUT THE AUTHOR

**ROB HAS BEEN FASCINATED** with plants since he was a child. As co-owner of Salisbury Greenhouse just outside of Edmonton, Alberta, he feels privileged to be able to share his passion with gardeners. He especially loves talking to gardeners who are just starting out and are eager to get their fingers dirty. His sense of inspiration is infectious, and he loves getting other people hooked on growing.

In his spare time, Rob writes poetry, climbs mountains in the Rockies, and works toward his Masters of Arts in Literature at the University of Alberta. He lives in Sherwood Park with his beloved wife Meg.